VENEZUELA

Westerners have lost the ability to reason!

LUÍS GARCIA

ISBN: 9781080607167
Independently published

Contributions by Claire Fighiera
Front cover image by Luís Garcia
Book design by Luís Garcia

First printing edition 2019

Nomadic Thoughts
nomadicthoughts.blogs.sapo.pt

We have to be radical, because we have to dig up our own roots. Radicals. That word has been demonized: "no, he is a radical", and they have assimilated it as the "madman". No, no, radical does not mean madman. I'm a radical. Radical, let's be radicals. Radical in our principles, well rooted, hence the word, from the "root" ["raíz" in Spanish]! Radical, radically revolutionary! Radically humanist! Radically patriots of Patria Grande [Great Fatherland]! Radically committed to life and to the people! Every day more and more radical!

Hugo Chávez

Where knowledge is a duty, ignorance is a crime.

Tomas Paine

CONTENTS

HOW TO USE THIS BOOK

This book offers plenty of descriptions of historical events and facts unknown by the overwhelming majority of the people living in what the author labels as the "Western world". These historical events and facts are in total contradiction with the accepted narrative on Venezuela, especially in the "Western World".

Aware of this fact, the author decided to create a website where the readers can access plenty of sources confirming the apparently odd narrative contained in this book.

This book can be easily read without consulting the data provided on the website.

Nevertheless, the author's advice is for the reader to check the sources for all the facts he/she didn't know or believed not to be true.

The data is organized by chapters and the website was designed to simplify the task of reading the book while having instant access to footage and all sorts of data (on a laptop or other device).

Website: https://bookvenezuela.blogs.sapo.pt

DEMOCRACY

16.03.2019

What kind of neural short-circuit hit most Western minds to make them swallow absurd and nonsensical lies like the ones we've witnessed lately? It seems that there are millions of Europeans out there living in a world where people in Brussels force them to choose between kind austerity and brutal austerity, and - what the hell-, those Europeans still believe they live in "democracy"!

For instance, look at Portugal, the country where I was born. In a total and undemocratic violation of the poor Portuguese constitution, the European constitution (written by who knows who) has been imposed on the Portuguese people, and apparently, it has the magical power of passing over the Portuguese constitution, which was written and approved by the Portuguese people. Sure, the Constitutional Treaty was never ratified, but someone came up with the Treaty of Lisbon, a piece of Orwellian reformulations used to impose the very same European Constitution that was refused by the people of certain nations who had the opportunity to vote against it in a referendum. And yes, eventually, the Treaty of Lisbon was enforced undemocratically!

A European Commission and a President of the European Commission who were not elected by the European people, take ignominious decisions on how to steal, abuse and enslave the Portuguese people without even asking them whether they think it is right or not to have metaphoric hot irons shoved in certain metaphoric openings of their bodies.

And, if by any chance, the Portuguese people dare to complain about their metaphoric charred sphincters, the "democratic" leaders in Brussels will immediately order their puppets in Lisbon to shut them up, making them be sure that everything is decided "democratically", according to the non-voted European Constitution which unconstitutionally has the "right" to pass over the raped Portuguese constitution.

*

Then, imagine this: Portuguese people *enlightened* by plenty of televised Western electromagnetic waves that, combined, burn

2

both their eyes and their brains, making them believe Venezuela is a "dictatorship" and Maduro is a "dictator".

Well, first of all, it seems that Portuguese (and other Western) sheep-like humans have lost the ability to read because there's no shortage of good and free Portuguese dictionaries. In a dictatorship, there must be someone dictating without asking and without having been elected.

But Maduro was elected!

And the Venezuelan elections, for many years, have been the ones welcoming the highest numbers of accredited international observers (including imperialist Europeans and imperialist Yankees). And none of them have ever found a serious fault or problem during any Venezuelan election. Facts are facts, and can easily be checked online.

The last presidential elections took place more than half a year ago and, until January 2019, the *Western sheep-like humans* had nothing to say about it, since they never have a fucking idea of what goes on in Venezuela, except when Western Lying Media tell them to believe they "know" something or to be "concerned" about something.

They don't know and never wished to know that the opposition coalition (clearly funded by the EU and the US, in an glaring example of interference of that very same kind the pathetic West falsely accuses Russia of carrying out in the US and Europe), in 2017, was betting that Maduro would not let presidential elections take place in 2018.

They do not know that this coalition even wanted to anticipate the elections, believing that they could easily win them.

They do not know that the opposition coalition lost face when, with a majority in the parliament (by the way, since when, in a dictatorship, the parliament can be controlled by the opposition?), they passed an amnesty law[1] in which in which can be found an official admission of their past crimes. As Kevin Zeese and Margaret Flowers rightly pointed out[2]:

"In 2016, the economic crisis led to the opposition winning a majority in the National Assembly. One of their first acts was to pass an amnesty law. The law described 17 years of crimes including violent felonies and terrorism committed by the opposition. It was an admission of crimes back to the 2002 coup and through 2016. The law demonstrated violent treason against Venezuela. One month later, the Supreme Court of Venezuela ruled the amnesty law was unconstitutional. US media, regime change advocates and anti-Venezuela human rights groups attacked the Supreme Court decision, showing their alliance with the admitted criminals.

Years of violent protests and regime change attempts, and then admitting their crimes in an amnesty bill, have caused those opposed to the Bolivarian Revolution to lose power and become unpopular. In three recent elections Maduro's party won regional, local and the Constituent Assembly elections."

They do not know that, after having miserably failed in their anti-democratic attempts to sabotage the 2017 constitutional revision convened by Maduro, the opposition coalition completely broke down. Some of the member parties of the coalition did not want to further damage their public image, knowing that sabotaging an election and a referendum are precisely the kind of actions one should avoid when trying to improve its own public image.

They do not know that, after the opposition coalition broke down, all these opposition parties were sure they would never have a chance to win presidential elections running separately and, as a result, most of them decided not to participate. But yes, the elections were held in 2018, as planned, proving Venezuela is a democracy.

They do not know that most opposition parties voluntarily boycotted the elections and, therefore, they have no right to complain about the results.

They do not know that Maduro won the elections with 67.8% of the votes, against Henri Falcón (20.9%) and Javier Bertucci (10.8%).

They do not know that the Venezuelan opposition does not even complain about the electoral procedure. The opposition did not complain now nor complained at the time (May 2018). What we have is Guaidó and his US-sponsored gang "arguing" that the elections were "illegitimate" because they were called by a Constituent Assembly[3] (convened by Maduro) and not by the National Assembly (Parliament of Venezuela) - what a nonsense -, and ridiculously complaining that some convicted criminals (like Leopoldo López or Henrique Capriles) were prevented from participating in those elections - what a nonsense too.

*

Just read the Venezuelan constitution (democratically approved by the Venezuelan people) and confirm by yourself that nothing went wrong with the presidential elections.

On the contrary, first, Maduro just fulfilled his duty by calling for new presidential elections. Strange "dictatorship" in which the "dictator" calls for presidential elections, isn't it true dear westerners?

Second, as provided by the country's Constitution, logically, when a constituent assembly is formed (to revise the current Constitution), the parliament is temporarily closed, as it cannot possibly legislate using a core set of laws in process of revision.

Third, Maduro calling for new elections proves that he respects the Venezuelan Constitution and the democratic institutions. If he hadn't called it, then he could be labeled as a dictator fearing electoral defeats and trying to undemocratically remain in power.

*

So, dear westerners, please tell me what kind of nonsense do you propose to object to the last presidential elections? Nothing, of course. And worse, even though no one in the opposition complains about the results (Maduro 67.8%, Falcón (20.9%), Bertucci 10.8%), apparently (from what I read online) most westerners really believe that this is what the opposition actually complains about. Wrong. So wrong. So painfully wrong.

Westerners, *poisoned* with pathetic and foolish ignorance, show empathy towards the *opposition* for what it hasn't even said!

It's sadly comic, but it's true.

*

Moreover, contrary to the obscure and almost superstitious Western beliefs, Venezuela is far more democratic than most Western countries. Since the 1999 Bolivarian Revolution, more than 20 elections have been held. The ruling party and its leaders won almost all of them and democratically respected the ones they lost. And, if they have lost a few, it means they have democracy, don't they?

In the middle of this criminal and genocidal economic war the vile West has been inflicting on the non-submissive Venezuela, a considerable part of its population bought the Western "regime change" propaganda (just like what happened in Allende's Chile, Mossaddegh's Iran, Goulart's Brazil or in Cuba over the last dozens of years: the Machiavellian U.S. admittedly attacking the economy of a country to turn its people against their rulers) and, *worse,* they elected an opposition coalition to run the parliament!

What kind of "dictatorship" allows the opposition to rule over the parliament? What kind of "dictator" does not have *wonderful ideas such as killing and torturing tens of thousands of civilians as Pinochet did in Chile, or bombing the parliament as Yeltsin did in Russia, or committing genocide, killing millions, as Sukarno did in Indonesia?*

No, strange "dictator" Maduro did nothing similar. Moreover, Maduro took an *astonishing* and democratic decision and respected the people's vote! And now what dear *Western sheep-like humans?* Are you sure you still want to call Maduro a "dictator"?

*

More, on December 2, 2007, Hugo Chávez's government was defeated in its proposal of a constitutional revision in which the Venezuelan people were invited to decide whether they wanted or not a limit of two consecutive terms (in the case of Germany's eternal

6

Merkel, there's no limit). At that time, the manipulative and deceitful Western media accused Chávez of being a dictator willing to perpetuate himself in power. What a joke! Chávez's proposal didn't pass but, obviously, Chávez and his party respected the people's will... and life went on!

Wow, what an amazing *dictator*! Instead of forcefully staying in power forever and silence the people with Pinochet-like abductions, use of torture and death... no, *bloody* Chávez convened a referendum! And his proposal was refused! And he accepted the results! Oh man, what an *amazing dictator*!

Nevertheless, it is very common to hear westerners saying they don't know anything about what is happening and that they are too confused! Of course they are, what were they expecting?

They self-inflict a total 24/7 censorship on all the freely available facts... and then they *are surprised* by the fact that they can't understand what is going on in Venezuela?

And then, to fix it, they self-inject propaganda coming from the very same media that always lie about everything?

Confused? Doubtful? Oh, come on, give me a break! I bet their real problem is self-inflicted and desired ignorance, as well as good doses of cognitive dissonance. But sure, I might be wrong. Please, just prove me wrong!

*

Moreover, Venezuela is surely more democratic than Europe, as we can see from certain democratic options they have and we have not. In Venezuela, it's possible to put an end to a democratically elected government if enough signatures are collected.

I bet you will say that, if the necessary signatures were collected, the regime would not resign! Wrong again.

In 2004, when Chávez was president and, despite the fact that many of the signatures collected were not valid (10 times the same ID number, signatures of deceased people, etc.), the recall referendum[4] went on and... Chávez won again.

Chávez got an even greater result, showing that his honesty and respect for the democratic institutions (which he helped establish) were rewarded with a greater and firmer turnout by his supporters!

Meanwhile, in the United States, to become president, one must be a billionaire or a professional streetwalker... what a *nice* "democracy"!

DICTATORSHIP
17.03.2019

Strange "dictatorship" in which the Parliament is controlled by the opposition.

Strange "dictatorship" where elections are held all the time.

Strange "dictatorship" in which "dictators" lose elections and respect the results.

Strange "dictatorship" in which some can appeal, live on TV, to crimes against the president and the country, often in total impunity.

Strange "dictatorship" in which the "leader" of the opposition gives live interviews to dozens of anti-government private media, in public streets and in public places, without suffering any consequences.

Strange "dictatorship" where there are opposition parties.

Strange "dictatorship" in which these parties can organize illegal parallel elections, as they did in the summer of 2017, without suffering any consequences.

Strange "dictatorship" where the opposition controls almost all media.

Strange "dictatorship" where the perpetrators of the 2002 coup against Chávez live free and use their freedom to organize more crimes against the government and betray their motherland.

Strange "dictatorship" in which TV channels and newspapers that called for the 2002 coup and directly participated in it, remain open and their owners free.

*

If you are an honest person now reading this article, and if you really seek the truth about what's going on in Venezuela, you can't afford to ignore documentaries like *The Revolution Will Not Be Televised* [1] or *The War on Democracy* [2]. These two and others more contain footage and pieces of evidence that are crucial to understand and to prove what I just wrote above.

But let's continue.

*

Strange "dictatorship" in which referendums are called all the time.

Strange "dictatorship" in which the opposition-controlled parliament gives itself the *pleasure* of sabotaging Maduro's government during its fight against the Imperial Economic War.

Strange "dictatorship" in which the opposition-controlled parliament calls for crimes against the motherland (calls for more sanctions and for more economic sabotage, even calls for foreign military intervention)!

Strange "dictatorship" in which the "peaceful opposition" can afford to kill policemen and pro-government civilians by shooting and bombing and burning them alive!

Source 3 - Terrorist "peaceful opposition" preparing to burn alive a pro-government "Chavista"

You can find more pieces of evidence of those crimes in my article: *Venezuela for dummies*[4].

You can find *tons* of pieces of evidence in free e-books (in PDF) like:

- *Venezuela se respecta - Derechos humanos en revolución* [5]
- *Venezuela se respeta - Universidades víctimas de la barbarie* [6]
- *Venezuela se respeta* [7]
- *Víctimas de la Arrechera* [8]
- *Víctimas de la Guarimba* [9]
- *Víctimas fatales de la violencia política - Abril– Julio 2017*[10]

Even if you don't understand Spanish, please open the e-books above because, if you do so, you can access and analyze by yourself horrific proofs of the terror perpetrated by the opposition (never shown on Mainstream Lying Media).

Source 11 – Video showing Venezuelan police forces victims of a terrorist attack committed by the "opposition"

But the lobotomized Western sheep-like humans swallow the propaganda, swallow the Orwellian Minute of Hate Against Venezuela, and then they go to watch their soap operas or their favorite teams playing. Clichés? Yes, but clichés systematically confirmed by reality.

What they never do is to search, to analyze, to read articles like this one (or better ones), to read books like the ones I suggested, to watch documentaries like the ones I also suggested. And that's why many (good) people are wrong when they feel sad about their brainwashed Western friends. They are not exactly brainwashed and ignorant beings. No, in most cases, westerners are just not willing to acknowledge the dark painful reality. André Vltchek already said everything about this disturbing fact in his article *Western Public "Does Not Know", or "Does Not Want to Know"?*[12]

Strange "dictatorship" which put Leopoldo López under house arrest, who, after the electoral defeat in 2012, went to the streets, in public rallies, and openly appealed to violence against the government and invited his followers to "not wait another 6 years" (of Maduro's democratic mandate), but rather carry out crimes against the government and the nation! The same Leopoldo López who, in 2002, actively participated in the coup against Chávez!

Source 13 – one more documentary on the 2002 coup, about the attack against the Cuban Embassy (in Spanish)

Yet, most westerners accept all this dark comedy, poor sheep-like humans!

They accept it. They buy it. They swallow it. They cry for non-victims of crimes not committed by the Venezuelan government.

*

But they do not cry when Chilean women, victims of the dictator injected by the United States in Chile, get electric shocks on their vaginas and nipples!

They don't cry when Iraqi women are raped in front of their husbands.

They don't cry when Afghan civilians are shot to death by some psychopath US soldiers, just for the *fun* of it.

They do not cry for 12-year-old children indefinitely imprisoned in Guantánamo, in total violation of International Law and in total disregard for the human dignity of those children illegally abducted by the US machine of global terror!

They do not cry when 10-year-old girls are sold to Saudi pedophiles in Turkish markets, as a result of Western aggression on Syria!

They do not cry watching Africans being literally sold as slaves in Libyan slave markets, a country that used to be the richest and most developed African state, with a magnificent welfare state, before the French Terrorist Army and the British Terrorist Army came and raped Libya.

They do not cry when Syrian homosexuals are thrown from the top of buildings by the terrorist "opposition" funded by Western tax-payers.

They do not cry when hundreds of thousands of human beings in Papua (Indonesia) and millions of human beings in Congo are slaughtered in the name of Wild Western Capitalism.

No, I'm not accusing! I'm stating facts! Human beings are, right now, being chased like wild pigs, shot dead, massacred by Indonesian genocidal forces, so Australian, European and US companies can continue to plunder Papua in total impunity!

Western sheep-like humans, if they believe themselves to be true humanists, they should be fully aware of all these crimes. But they aren't.

They are never aware of the most grotesque crimes being committed by the West, all over the planet, at any given time.

They are always too busy crying for West-sponsored aggressors and too busy blaming the victims.

They are always too busy crying for nonexistent victims and nonexistent crimes fabricated by National Endowment for Democracy, Council on Foreign Relations, Albert Einstein Institute, Freedom House, International Republican Institute, National Democratic Institute, Hoover Institution, American Enterprise Institute, etc.

Worst, most westerners never heard about these "regime change" organizations I just mentioned, the reason why I insist to call them "sheep-like humans".

*

No way. They submissively and obediently cry for the terrorist Leopoldo López under house arrest in a luxury house, after having committed crimes which, if committed in the United States, would have brought him to an electric chair!

For them, Venezuela is a "dictatorship", but not France!

The French regime can hurt hundreds of demonstrators and savagely beat them up because Yellow Vests are all a "bunch of hooligans".

But Leopoldo López and his fellow terrorists in the "opposition" can call for criminal attacks against the Venezuelan "regime", can burn hospitals, universities or public transportation, and even bomb police forces, only to be left alone. If the Venezuelan authorities capture them, Venezuela is surely a "dictatorship oppressing peaceful demonstrators", right? That's it, dear westerners, that's it! Just as black is white, war is peace, and the sky is green! Baa...

Source 14 – Leopoldo López publicly calling for violence

Western sheep-like humans swallow it all and always ask for more. In 2012 they swallowed Leopoldo López, now they swallow Juan Guaidó. Make sure you Western sheep-like humans figuratively choke for good with both of them at once:

Source 15 – Picture of Leopoldo López and Juan Guaidó together, during a public meeting

But well, chapter 13 is dedicated to Juan Guaidó, The Unknown! For now, I will continue with the subject "dictatorship".

*

Let me think... Dictatorship... Saudi Arabia!

In Saudi Arabia, which does not even have a proper Constitution, and where women have fewer rights than pigs and cows (but "they can finally drive cars", right dear Western *progressive* beings?), and where peaceful protesters like the Shia cleric Nimr al-Nimr are beheaded in public squares... there westerners see no dictatorship at all and, therefore, they do not feel outraged by what the Saudi draconian regime does! Amazing!

Uncle Sam doesn't tell Western sheep-like humans to be outraged by all the crimes committed by one of the most barbaric, criminal and terrorist states on Earth (after Israel, the US, France, and the United Kingdom), so the average Western sheep-like human doesn't even think about Saudi Arabia. Come on, Uncle Sam has over $400 billion worth of weaponry to sell to Saudi Arabia over the next 10 years! Obedient westerners shall go to bed and try to fall asleep counting sheep in a mirror.

*

Let me think... Dictatorship... Indonesia!

In Indonesia, where millions of communists, atheists and Chinese were killed after the US-sponsored coup d'état in 1965, there, in that astonishing "democracy", it is illegal to be a communist or an atheist.

There you can find anti-communist museums.

There, left-wing parties cannot participate in the forthcoming elections.

There, right now, the very "democratic" local authorities are burning left-wing literature in public squares.

But westerners, because their Orwellian CNN, BBC, DW, and France24 tell them nothing about it, they find no reason to feel outraged! Nothing, nothing, absolutely nothing. After all, according to the Western Lying Media, Indonesia is a "normal" country. Absolutely "normal" oppression and "normal" dictatorship, right? Not sure? Read these essays written by André Vltchek[16]:

- *Filming in the Most Depressing City on Earth – Jakarta* [17]
- *Palangkaraya – Dreaming about the 'Soviet' Capital of Indonesia* [18]
- *Indonesian Tsunami – Thievery, Ineptness and Presidential Elections* [19]

*

Let me think... Dictatorship... Brazil!

Dilma Rousseff was unfairly removed from power, through a purely political process (and not legal, since Rousseff was not formally accused of anything). There, a dictatorship was installed, with Temer as president.

Temer was not elected, simply being a member of the party PSDB, one of the parties in the former ruling coalition. How did westerners manage to see "democracy" in a country that, during two years, was ruled by an unelected person whose party had a tiny percentage of popular support? No, seriously, have westerners lost the ability to reason?

*

Let me think... Dictatorship... USA!

The average westerner loves the US, or at least sympathizes with the US. The average westerner believes in the laughable cliché: "the US is the greatest democracy in the world".

Oh man, the biggest "democracy" in the world in which Afro-Americans are incarcerated by the millions just for being Afro-Americans; where these very same human beings work literally as slaves in private prisons, so rich owners of European *castes* can get their economic profits; where these human beings only leave their prisons to go risk their own lives fighting dangerous fires that nobody else dares to fight, being paid 30 cents an hour to do so!

"Democracy" in which one can be indefinitely arrested without formal charge (Patriot Act).

"Democracy" in which citizens are Orwellianly controlled and spied 24/7, everywhere, and in every possible and imaginable way.

"Democracy" in which only billionaires and professional streetwalkers can run for the presidency... And so on... What a *lovely* democracy!

*

And, by the way, what about France? Dictatorship? Oppression?

Repression? Anything?

I insist, democracy or dictatorship? Sure, Macron was elected, but so was Maduro!

In France, unarmed and peaceful protesters end up as hundreds of civilians violently injured, bombed or brutally beaten up by the French police forces (read *Overthrow the oppressive French regime!*[20] and *Overthrow the oppressive French regime! - Part 2*[21]). Meanwhile, in Venezuela, the wounded ones are policemen[22] and government's supporters[22].

Source 23 – French citizen seriously wounded
Source 24 – Unarmed citizen unnecessarily attacked with a hand grenade
Source 25 – Unarmed citizens savagely beaten up

*

No, dear westerners, really, how is it possible to see so little where there's so much and to see so much where there's nothing? How is it possible to be so illogical, irrational, biased, naive, confused, stunned, submissive and lamebrained? How is it possible to be indefinitely manipulated by the very same old lies?

No, dear not dear Western anti-journalists, how dare you to show images of Guaidó expressing himself freely, surrounded by dozens of cameras, microphones, and anti-government journalists, and then tell us that, in the Venezuelan "dictatorship", there's "repression" and lack of "freedom of expression"?

And what kind of seizures do you suffer from, dear Western sheep-like humans, that prevent you from realizing the absurdity of having BBC, CNN and other Western Media showing you images of Guaidó expressing himself freely, surrounded by dozens of cameras, microphones and anti-government journalists, to then tell you that, in the Venezuelan "dictatorship", there's "repression" and lack of "freedom of expression"?

What I would love to see is Shias from Saudi Arabia, or communists from Indonesia, or anti-dictatorship politicians from Thailand, giving public interviews as Guaidó does. And doing it without being whipped, arrested, tortured or beheaded! Do you get it, dear Western sheep-like humans?

Oh boy, what a "repression" they have there in Venezuela! Oh boy, what a "lack of freedom of expression" they endure there in Venezuela!

INFORMATION
19.03.2019

Millions can be seen, in photos and videos, supporting Maduro, the democratically elected Venezuelan President. If a westerner believes himself to be well informed by his Orwellian propaganda machine, can that westerner explain the reason why none of these images are shown in Western Lying Media?

And no, westerners cannot afford to say that all these lies and manipulated disinformation are the fault of Western Lying Media! Or the fault of Imperialism!

No, the fault is yours, Western sheep-like humans. You ask and beg to be deceived, over and over again!

As Noam Chomsky argues[1], we have now more propaganda and manipulation than ever before but, at the same time, never before we had so much information and such easy access to it. Therefore, the conclusion can only be one, a very simple one: the responsibility for this Orwellian situation we live in, in the West and its client states, lies on the intellectual laziness and on the hypocrisy of those willing to be deceived.

A great researcher and fearless freedom fighter, Professor Tim Anderson[2], sums this up very well in a single montage:

Source 3 – Sarcastic montage comparing French "democracy" with Venezuelan "dictatorship"

The populace watches the footage and then, unconsciously but also consciously, interprets it the way they were conditioned to interpret it.

The media tell them peaceful French demonstrators brutally beaten by deranged French policemen are "hooligans", and the populace concedes.

The media tell them that one of the countries with the highest levels of freedom of expression (freedom to even call for illegal coups or to call for the death of elected presidents) is a horrible repressive regime, and the populace concedes...

*

But let's go back to the crowds supporting Maduro and the Venezuelan government, democratically elected half a year ago. The democratic process and the immense support the Venezuelan people gave to Maduro, once again, has not been televised. The masters of Western manipulation willingly omitted all these facts and, as a natural consequence, the Western populace didn't notice the Bolivarian revolution moving forward.

I remember that in 2012, during the anti-government demonstrations in Portugal, there were, altogether, more than half a million persons. And what did the media tell us at that time? They told us it was nothing but a minority of lazy Portuguese troublemakers trying to screw things up instead of going to work.

If 500,000 persons out of 10.5 million represent a voiceless and lazy minority, what can be said about demonstrations with a few thousand anti-Maduro demonstrators (sometimes tens of thousands, on special occasions) in a population of 32 million Venezuelans? Is basic math failing in the West? Or is westerners' reasoning failing? I bet both are failing in Western submissive and gullible minds.

That's why they swallow figures of "80% of Venezuelans supporting Guaidó", scandalously made up by the Portuguese state channel RTP. Why tell the truth, and check it out, when one can make it up without suffering any consequences or without having the populace complaining about it, right? Very *good*, for the deceivers and the deceived ones! Bravo!

*

Now let's go back to the footage about Venezuela.

If tens of thousands of anti-Maduro protesters, out of 32 million inhabitants, are so important for RTP (and its fellow Western Lying Media), why was RTP not showing empathy towards 500,000 anti-government protesters (out of 10.5 million) in Portugal, back in 2012?

If tens of thousands of anti-Maduro protesters, out of 32 million inhabitants, are so appealing for Western consciences, why the hell doesn't the West show any interest for the many millions demonstrating in favor of Maduro's government?

Knowing that, in Portugal and in the rest of Europe, there's no shortage of internet connections to access *tons* of pictures and videos proving what I just stated, an honest person, fair and wise, is forced to conclude that: RTP, CNN, BBC, DW or France24 lie all the time. They lie, manipulate, hide and deceive on purpose. And the Western sheep-like humans swallow it, deeply, incredibly deep, because they are indeed sheep-like humans.

Look at these images showing millions of Maduro supporters (and don't tell me these images showing millions of pro-government supporters are "propaganda of the regime", otherwise I will answer: your images showing thousands of anti-government protesters are propaganda of the Western Imperial Regime):

Sources 4, 5 – Pictures of crowded pro-government protests
Sources 6, 7, 8 and 9 – Footage of crowded pro-government protests

No need to keep sharing what any person, intellectually decent, can easily find on their own with a mobile phone (or a PC) and a basic internet connection (Europe and North America are not exactly deserts like the Sahara, so there are no excuses).

Just take a look at Tim Anderson's Instagram account[10] and similar ones!

Just take a look at Abby Martin's Twitter account[11] and similar ones!

Just take a look at Grayzone channel[12] and other similar channels on

YouTube!

And, if you think you haven't seen enough footage of pro-Maduro protesters, please take your time and check the content of articles published by Venezuelanalysis[13]. Here's a wonderful example: *In Images: Venezuelan People Mobilize In Support of Maduro*[14].

Or look at the footage published by Telesur in articles such as: *Marcha bolivariana en frontera con Brasil: "Venezuela es un pueblo de guerreros"*[15].

No, there's no excuse! As Vltchek[16] wrote:

> "It is not because the public in the West 'doesn't know', but because it does everything it can in order not to know. Or if it knows or suspects, it makes sure to act as if it is ignorant. For its own selfish interests. For its own privileges."

*

A true journalist has to show both sides of a story in the most impartial way possible.

But the prostituted Western Lying Media do, with Venezuela, what they have been doing for years with Syria:

They show recycled images (of Palestinians massacred by Zionists to portray alleged massacres of civilians by the Syrian Arab Army).

They completely censor all the footage showing hundreds and thousands of Syrians civilians and Syrian soldiers savagely tortured and massively executed by the terrorist "rebels" armed by the West and financed by Western taxpayers.

I have shared this kind of content dozens of times in my articles. Read and analyze the articles, if you feel like it.

Journalism that chooses a side and only shows that side,

makes things up, lies, manipulates, and cheats, like in the cases of BBC and CNN, is not journalism! It's propaganda, Orwellian propaganda!

Self-respecting Western journalists should read the *Munich Declaration of the Duties and Rights of Journalists*[17] and try to respect it, doing the exact opposite of what they have been doing in their coverage of the Western Aggression on Venezuela.

Self-respecting Western journalists should not ignore the constant massacre of Syrian civilians by the savage US Army.

Self-respecting Western journalists should not ignore the terrorist chemical attacks committed by the US Army in Syria, like the recent one that killed 50 civilians:

Source 18 – Footage of a terrorist chemical attack delivered by the US Army in Syria

Self-respecting Western journalists should stop reporting events that never took place, like the made-up chemical attack in Douma, Syria. Many others and I said so, and proved so: it never happened. Now, almost a year later, some Western media are finally admitting it was staged[19].

Self-respecting Western journalists should not ignore the fact that more than 10 million Yemenis are being literally starved to death and that an entire country (Yemen) is being criminally destroyed by the US, the UK, the UAE and Saudi Arabia when, at the same time, they are reporting some thousands of Venezuelans suffering from "hunger" (read: limited access to food due to Western sanctions and embargoes, the very same set of countries guilty of starving Yemenis to death, the very same set of countries willing to deliver "humanitarian aid" to the starving Venezuelans). On this topic alone, Western Lying Media raped half of the Munich Declaration.

*

And then, think about it, dear westerners: why don't Western Media show pro-Macron protests in France? Because it's almost impossible to find such a thing, right? Right!

Almost all those protesting in France, do it against Macron and not for Macron. Hundreds of them have savagely been wounded and beaten up. Yet, the prostituted Western Media do not mention any oppression or repression or lack of freedom of expression there, and they even dare to say anti-Macron protesters "disrespect the French democratic order"! They are the beaten ones, but they are the ones disrespecting the democratic order? How come?

Basically, there are only anti-Macron protesters in France. If we were to believe Western Media, we could conclude: there are only anti-Maduro protesters in Venezuela. In that case, we would have 2 countries with people protesting against their leaders. In a world with reasoning human beings, obviously, both conflicts should be treated equally. Unless one side was worse than the other. And yes, anti-Maduro protesters burn people alive and destroy hospitals and universities. No doubt they are the worst!

Moreover, unlike in France, in Venezuela, there are anti and pro-government protesters. Even assuming they have equal numbers (which they don't, the pro-government protesters in Venezuela outnumber by far the anti-government protesters), the only conclusion an honest journalist could possibly come up with would be: what a great democracy, where there's room for different and even opposite perspectives!

But the truth is: Western Lying Media see nothing wrong about France savagely oppressing its people, while they call Venezuelan government an "oppressive regime", knowing it has immense peaceful support in a country where the outnumbered opposition endlessly commits clear acts of savage terrorism. In conclusion, Western Lying Media support savagery and terror!

Source 20 - French policemen savagely beating up unarmed civilians

In Venezuela, where pro-government protests have dozens of times more participants than anti-government protests, there are no Western journalists to film the very frequent pro-government protests.

In Venezuela, yes, there are huge crowds of pro-government protesters calling for peace, asking the government to put an end to violent anti-government protests, to put an end to anti-government vandalism and to put an end to the attacks against the democratic order perpetrated by anti-government protesters.

But in this case, in a very illogical manner, and in clear violation of the Munich Declaration, the prostituted Western Media have nothing to say against vandals disrespecting the democratic order! Can someone explain to me why? Are Western "journalists" covering Venezuela, or are they agents of manipulation working for the Western propaganda machine? I think the answer is obvious.

Source 21 - Terrorist Venezuelan opposition bombing Venezuelan policemen

Did you watch it? Yes? So think about it. Does it make sense to say French civilians are just troublemakers and Venezuelan people are oppressed?

No, it doesn't.

Yet, this dystopian situation is not the fault of Western propagandists. No! It's the fault of Western sheep-like humans who do not realize the deception because they have lost the ability to reason. And because they actually have reasons to prefer to be deceived, therefore avoiding the inconvenient truth: their high standards of living are supported by the plunder and rape of the rest of the world, including, if possible, Venezuela!

*

Western media say that the majority of Venezuelans supports the non-candidate non-elected Guaidó, and the Western sheep-like humans buy it. Math? Facts? Logic? Who cares!

In the West, nobody cares. In the very same West directly responsible for the Venezuelan crisis", westerners only care about one side, the side their governments and elites funded and helped create, shamelessly interfering in the internal affairs of a sovereign nation. And Western media only give voice to that discredited side.

In the West, nobody wants to know; nobody wants to inform.

If I'm wrong, why does no one show pictures of pro-Maduro protesters burned-alive and killed, public universities completely destroyed or tons of food burned? Why? Because all these crimes were committed by the beloved criminals you call "opposition", right dear westerners? So, where's the wonderful Western freedom of information?

Private cars burning in Paris are examples of crimes caused by "vandalism"; entire public universities, public hospitals and public subway stations burning in Caracas are great achievements of your "freedom fighting" protesters, right? What do you mean? Freedom in the sense of getting rid of what socialism has to offer? I see...

*

Images and videos of terrorism perpetrated by anti-Maduro "protesters":

Source 22 - Attempt to burn alive a pro-government citizen
Source 23 - Orlando Figuera burned alive by "peaceful" opposition demonstrators
Source 24 - Orlando Figuera burned alive by "peaceful" opposition demonstrators
Source 25 - "Peaceful" protesters launching rockets
Source 26 - "Peaceful" protesters burning and destroying 50 tons of food
Source 27 - "Peaceful" protesters destroying and burning voting machines
Source 28 - Two Venezuelan policemen beaten and then forced to walk naked by

the "peaceful" opposition
Source 29 - "Peaceful" opposition cutting down trees to block streets

*

But let's go back, once again, to the "information" produced by Western "journalists". If they create "information" and not propaganda, why do they take a side? Don't they know that information is supposed to be impartial? And don't you know that information is supposed to be impartial? Can you notice how biased is the Western "information"? Why can't westerners reason logically and stop buying Western MSM propaganda?

The Western media are openly and shamelessly cheering for a US coup in Venezuela! And they only speak to criminals without ever explaining their criminal past.

And there's worse, there are even those who change their profile photo on Twitter and Facebook, as Reuters did some weeks ago, as The Economist did, that pitiful neoliberal propaganda pamphlet that spends its time attacking the real left in Venezuela (truly socialist, revolutionary and democratic left):

Source 30 – screenshot of The Economist's Twitter account

How *lovely*! A Yankee media interfering with the Venezuelan democracy, clearly supporting Guaidó and comparing him to the Statue of Liberty (Statue of Slavery?). Then tell us stories about RT! Tell us that RT's hyper-rational analyses about the Orwellian reality people endure in the US are synonymous of "Russian interference!" Sure... not!

*

In conclusion, "information" in the West is outrageously untruthful, manipulative, biased; it's in love with Western terrorism; it lives or

29

survives thanks to ads that, in one way or the other, are also published to manipulate the populace. And all this goes on while Western MSM collect their millions of euros and dollars painted red, with the blood of Yemenis, Libyans, Syrians, Afghans, Venezuelans, and so many others.

Westerners have the right not to watch advertising propaganda or pseudo-journalistic propaganda, but they insist on doing so. They insist on willing to be deceived and manipulated. Otherwise, there's no lack of great journalistic work produced by honest human beings, absolutely committed to human dignity and life. I give you here some suggestions of books to read:

Eduardo Galeano:
Open Veins of Latin America: Five Centuries of the Pillage of a Continent [31]

Noam Chosmky:
What Uncle Sam Really Wants [32]

Naomi Klein:
The Shock Doctrine [33]

Ignácio Ramonet:
La tyrannie de la communication [34] (in French)

Luis Britto Garcia:
Dictatura Mediática en Venezuela - Investigación de unos medios por encima de toda sospecha [35] (in Spanish)

LIES AND DECEPTION AT THE BORDER

28.03.2019

As if this Machiavellian recipe to commit crimes in total impunity hadn't been used and reused over and over again, and while the victims are always the ones being blamed for the inflicted crimes (Daraa, Syria, 2011; Kyiv, Ukraine, 2014, etc.), the US decides to use in Venezuela the very same recipe of:

- Committing crimes against a weaker state, which, precisely because it is weak and threatened with a military invasion by the US, would never commit the crimes they are accused of (it would be suicidal);
- Ordering the Western Lying Media to manipulate footage and, while showing true images, reverse the narrative (Western Lying Media also do it voluntarily);
- Hoping that the local forces, in the exercise of their duty to contain the imposed violence, will be forced to injure or kill someone, so that the US can obtain the "humanitarian reason" to intervene.
- If the US can't obtain that "humanitarian reason" to intervene (that is, if local forces do not respond physically to prevent the destruction of public property or even the death of police officers, as it happened in Ukraine in 2014), US, Israeli or local snipers will probably receive orders to kill dozens of people (Venezuela 2002, Syria 2011, Ukraine 2014, etc.).

On the subject of the deaths in Venezuela caused by CIA-sponsored sniper attacks in 2002, read the book *Abril Golpe Adentro* [1] (in Spanish) and watch the documentary *Llaguno Bridge - Keys to a Massacre* [2].

The amazing thing is that, no matter how many times the US repeats this barbaric and criminal recipe, Western sheep-like humans swallow it without thinking, without questioning, without asking if it makes sense, without asking if there are factual pieces of evidence of what BBC or CNN tell them!! No, Western sheep-like humans say "baa" and they move on, absolutely sure that Chávez, Yanukovych or Assad ordered the killing of peaceful civilians!

And the Western sheep-like humans do not notice that, as in Benghazi (Libya) or Daraa (Syria) or recently in Nicaragua, it is the "peaceful protests" (criminals paid by the American interference) that provoke armed conflicts:

Source 3 - Masked men shooting at the border of Venezuela and Colombia

But well, look at them the Western sheep-like humans, insisting on saying "baa"; look at them, closing their eyes for real crimes and real suffering. Western sheep-like humans are so away from reality and are so sure CNN, BBC or DW tells them The Truth that, while gullibly swallowing anti-Venezuela propaganda, they have no idea of the manslaughter US and its allies are committing right now in Yemen!

Source 4 - We support the Yemeni people against the crimes of the Saudi coalition
Source 5 - Charter for Compassion – Yemen
Source 6 - Propagated fake news vs untold-reality

If a picture is worth a thousand words, a video is worth many thousand more. Footage of the horrific reality Yemenis live in is never shown on Western MSM. Of course many can't handle shocking graphic content but, in a world where staged scenes of gruesome horror (like in Game of Thrones) help to normalize and even romanticize violence, and given the worldwide acceptance of Game of Thrones' graphic violence, it shouldn't be hard to find conscious human beings ready to watch real footage of Yemenis suffering[7, 8, 9, 10, 11, 12]. But it is indeed hard to find such human beings.

Back to the Western sheep-like humans, they have no idea about the massacres taking place right now in West Papua (Indonesia).

And Western MSM tells us absolutely nothing about fallen brave men like Yustinus Murib, a Papuasian leader who fought for the freedom of his people, killed and displayed as a hunting trophy by the genocidal and barbaric Indonesian Armed Forces:

Source 13 – picture of Murib displayed as a hunting trophy by Indonesian soldiers

Westerners know nothing about the systematic massacre of human beings in Papua because they don't want to know anything and because they lost the ability to reason. These supposed "humanitarian champions" prefer to support nonexistent causes and to close their eyes and brains to all the crimes against humanity perpetrated by their own countries (Western interventions in Libya, Syria, Afghanistan, Iraq, Honduras, Venezuela, etc.).

But, in truth, no, they are not humanists, and they have absolutely no empathy for human beings being tortured, beaten up, raped, enslaved, slaughtered, almost trampled as ants, from Congo to Papua, from Yemen to Libya, from Bahrain to Nigeria.

Westerners are not humanists and, apparently, they don't know what "empathy" is, given the fact that, when some stubborn *monster* like me mentions true genocides happening somewhere, this *monster* hears them saying "I don't have time for this" or "that's not my problem", or "we can do nothing", or "it is too far away from here", or "they are black" or "Asians, who cares". Basically, what most Westerners really mean, when they pronounce this kind of nonsense is: *Let them all die, I don't give a shit about non-westerners or non-Caucasians suffering and dying!*

Wrongly and foolishly, westerners only feel "sad" for what their beloved Big Brother orders them to "feel". And, poor them, they are so gullible, so spongy for emotional quibbling, so receptive for the simplest and dumbest propaganda ever made!

Westerners know nothing about true massacres and true crimes against humanity because they refuse to search, to investigate and to read/see/hear the *tons* of data available about all those crimes and massacres! Westerners refuse independent journalism produced by honest and committed people (like John Pilger[14]) who risk their own lives to inform us about real human suffering systematically censored or omitted by Western Lying Media.

That's why most westerners never read and will never read essays like *Southeast Asia Terribly Damaged but Lauded by the West* [15], in which André Vltchek informs us that:

"In West Papua – hundreds of thousands of people have already died, also under the Indonesian genocidal occupation, which is fully supported by the West, because Papua, like Borneo (which is known in Indonesia as Kalimantan) is getting thoroughly plundered by multi-national companies, of course under the careful supervision of Indonesian military forces. Horrors like the state-sponsored 'trans-migration' policy, designed to make people of Papua a minority on their own island, are ongoing and relentless. The people, who have lost everything under the occupation, are forced to convert to Islam, and they are also forced to abandon their way of life and their land. What Indonesia does in West Papua is nothing less than genocide. It is not only the killing and rape, of which its military could be accused of. The plunder of Papuan resources is as deadly for many other reasons, it is like if the force would be used to 'open up' vast parts of the Amazonia or Orinoco basins in South America – areas inhabited by indigenous tribes that have never come in contact with the outside world. Even the most insane right-wing presidents of Brazil or Venezuela (of the past), would never dream about such brutal genocidal undertakings (although this may change under the fascist presidency of Bolsonaro in Brazil). In West Papua, dozens of fragile cultures are disappearing. People who have never come into contact with the 'outside world' are being forced out of their rainforest, as trees are cut down and mining companies, backed by the Indonesian armed forces, ransack the land. Defenseless tribal people are dying from diseases and hunger, at the same time as corrupt Indonesian officials and businessmen are burning money in Jakarta's overprized malls, as well as in Singapore, Macau and Hong Kong. And now, thousands of Western tourists fly into West Papua, to Raja Ampat, which is becoming an 'in place' for diving!"

*

Let's go back to the recipe. If westerners had read the book I mentioned above, and if they had watched the documentaries I suggest in this book, and had applied logical reasoning to their research, I wouldn't need to add anything else.

Since 2013 (the beginning of the full-scale economic war on Venezuela), many researchers and alternative journalists have been publishing articles and essays with plenty of evidence, documents and arguments that can easily debunk and totally destroy, once and for all, the monstrous propaganda campaign waged against Venezuela, the horrific terrorist attacks against Venezuelans and the very economic war on Venezuela.

But no, just like with the coup in Ukraine 2014, the westerners are willing to be deceived and are anti-*humanitarianly* ready to support terrorists and accuse their victims of being "terrorists":

Source 16 – Ukranian police forces violently attacked by "peaceful" opposition

Policemen attacked and burned with flammable military substances which flames can't be extinguished, while the aggressors were "protesting peacefully" against the democratically elected "dictator" already at the end of his term.

Beating, gazing, kicking and punching policemen who were trying to protect public property in a passive manner... and the Western sheep-like humans saw a regime oppressing "peaceful protesters"? How? But yes, Western sheep-like humans did swallow this shitty manipulation. Yes, they did!

Do you want to see more? Here's more:

Source 17 – Ukranian police forces violently attacked by "peaceful" opposition

More here[18] and here[19]. There is not lack of footage of "peaceful protesters" (supported by Obama's terrorist regime, as John McCain and Victoria Nuland proved and admitted) injuring and killing "oppressive" Ukrainian policemen.

And now compare it with what just happened at the border between Colombia and Venezuela:

Yes, always the same. French policemen torturing and injuring peaceful protesters, and shooting "rubber bullets" at point-blank range to kill, and attacking unarmed civilians with grenades... all of this is reported as French uncivilized hooligans misbehaving and burning stuff, even when the images show the precise opposite. No matter what is going on in France, the Western Lying Media will tell the opposite and the *Western sheep-like humans* will swallow it.

Source 21 – French policemen torturing peaceful protesters
Source 22 – French policemen threatening to shoot protesters at a very short distance
Source 23 – French policeman attacking unarmed civilian with a grenade

In Venezuela, pro-coup thugs spreading gasoline over the trucks of supposed humanitarian aid, buildings, and bridges, and attacking and injuring the police forces with Molotov cocktails, grenades, and fire... and the pathetic Western Lying Media call it "confrontations" and "incidents"!

No, really, just look at what has been happening at the border with Colombia:

Sources 24, 25 – Opposition-staged operations, in an effort to blame Venezuela's government

And now what, dear Western sheep-like humans, who were confronting who? The footage clearly shows that the police acted in a passive manner and did not confront anybody, only tried to protect public property. The footage clearly shows that some Venezuelan thugs were the only ones attacking and destroying!

Where's that damn "confrontation"? I can't find it. Western Lying Media reported some 300 injured and 4 dead. Sure, but whose fault?

If it were the police's fault, and if the Western media could prove it, Western Media would surely spend the next few months showing the alleged pieces of evidence. If they don't show it, it's because they don't have anything to show. In fact, they don't even accuse the police directly (Because they know the police forces are innocent, right?)! No, they only imply lies (police fault) and omit real facts (opposition's fault).

As always, if the Western Media don't talk about the responsibility for the deaths and injuries, it is because they know the injuries and deaths were originated by the savage acts of the terrorist "opposition", to whom they provide full anti-journalistic support, just as happened during the 2013-14 terrorist "protests" in Venezuela)!

Amazing how Western Lying Media can call these deaths a result of the "oppression" inflicted by the "regime" upon its people! And even more amazing is that human beings in the West, alive and breathing normally, believe such pathetic propaganda.

And if they show a "martyr" of the regime, burnt out, poor him, they deliberately "forget" to inform you that the *poor guy* burned himself while spreading gasoline over trucks (of supposed humanitarian aid) set on fire by the same "martyr" and his fellow terrorists.

Western Lying Media also *forgot* to conclude that, if there are *tons* of images of "peaceful" protesters throwing Molotov cocktails, grenades and rockets against the police and setting trucks on fire with gasoline, the "regime" can never be blamed for what happened and, in this case, the "martyr" is not a martyr but a criminal!

And they forget to apologize to the Venezuelan government for slandering it so shamelessly. And to apologize to the public for lying to them so shamelessly when they accused the "regime" of having *produced* a "martyr".

And they forget to apologize and admit that there are no images of police attacking anyone with fire, but being attacked with fire, so that, to speak of a "martyr of the regime all burnt", is like talking about Vanuatu *winning* the World Cup... and not mention the 5 Brazilian titles!

Western sheep-like humans do not draw their own conclusions based on what their eyes witness because, inside their brains, there's no data processing. Otherwise, they would realize that there are no confrontations in Venezuela. And if there are injured people, it is because the "opposition" uses hazardous materials to protest "peacefully", materials such as grenades and rockets, and they set trucks on fire with gasoline, and they might use military chemicals that, when set on fire, the fire produced can't be extinguished, as we witnessed during the EuroMaidan (And I wonder where do they get military chemicals from? From China? From Russia? Or rather from NATO members, the ones now threatening to invade Venezuela?

Source 27 – Evidence of false flags in Venezuela

But well, for the Western media, it's all confrontation and oppression; vague "violence" and vague "incidents", without ever being pointing fingers to the real criminals (the "opposition"). By default, Western Lying Media simply concluded that were the Venezuelan authorities the ones who set fire to the trucks of "humanitarian aid".

Not a single word about what usually comes inside the trucks with "humanitarian aid" provided by the same country openly supporting the criminal Venezuelan "opposition". The same US that usually brings weapons and ammunition inside their trucks of "humanitarian aid", as we witnessed in 2016 in Aleppo.

No, no explanations, no historical comparisons. Only close-ups of burning trucks, to avoid showing the true criminals and to prevent the Western sheep from noticing that the trucks were burning on the Colombian side of the border!

Source 28 – Aid trucks burned by opposition gangs to blame Maduro.

And no mention of the fact that Venezuelan policemen were seriously attacked by thugs on the Colombian side, being Colombia a US client state where the US has several military bases.

Western media omitted many important facts. Yet, there was no shortage of Western journalists on the Colombian side of the border. For sure they know who set the trucks on fire. For sure they witnessed the Venezuelan police forces forming passive *human shields* to protect public property and the national territory while being attacked with fire coming from the Colombian side!

How come westerners don't see what the footage shows?

No, seriously, go to London or Washington and attack the police forces with Molotov cocktails, grenades or rockets. Attack the House of Lords or the White House with all that and kill some British or American policemen. Then let me know how it ended up! And do not forget to order Western media to call you "a peaceful protester", to define your terrorist attacks as "protests", to call "oppressors working for the regime" to the police officers you wounded or killed and, finally, to conclude that what happened there were mere "incidents" and clashes".

Seriously, if you truly swallow the journalistic trash the Western Lying Media have been feeding you with... go on, do it yourself in your own country. Copy-paste what has been done by "peaceful protesters" at the border between Colombia and Venezuela. Good luck with that!

*

Back to the Western journalists, please show me a single image of the Venezuelan police forces mistreating peaceful protesters or kindly shut up! Look at what is happening in France, and then show me something of the kind, if you can, occurred in Venezuela under Maduro or Chávez! Good luck!

Go ahead, try to find a video or photo of Venezuelan policemen savagely beating defenseless civilians as we see every day in the "democratic" terrorist state known as France:

Source 29 – French policemen savagely beating defenseless civilians

In the meantime, I'll show you how the American police forces treat civilians in their country. Look here[30], here[31] and here[32], and a playlist here[33], in case the reader is not aware or convinced about the systematic abuse of force by the US police forces.

If the Western sheep-like humans were not the brainwashed puppets they are, they could use something they use every day (YouTube) and find that there are thousands of videos available showing the Orwellian oppressive forces of the Yankee regime beating and sometimes even killing unarmed civilians, peaceful protesters, etc.

Or showing barbaric "Syrian" jihadists financed by Western tax-payers torturing Syrian civilians or massacring hundreds of Syrian soldiers at once.

Or showing Yemeni schools bombed by Saudi Arabia with the help of the United Kingdom and the same USA that "wants" to deliver "humanitarian aid" to embargoed and attacked Venezuela (that, by the way, already received 933 tons of true humanitarian aid[34], with no preconditions, from China, Russia, Cuba, and other countries).

Yes, Western sheep-like humans behave like brainless puppets! Damn it!

Poor Western puppets who swallow the shitiest calls for barbarism! They have lost their ability to reason! In the 21st century of fiber-optic, internet and smartphones, somehow, they can't see the blatant barbarism that takes place in the USA, Indonesia or Saudi Arabia. They don't see it because they were not told to see it and because they also do not want to see it!

Westerners, if they had a minimum of decency, common sense and humanism, they would read John Pilger's articles like *The war on Venezuela is built on lies* [35].

But most westerners, who had such characteristics, already lost them all... The topic of the day, for a Western sheep-like human, is what the MSM daily impose, using hyper-sensationalist and figurative hammers to figuratively smash their empty real heads.

41

Western sheep-like humans don't analyze nor discern anything. All they understand nowadays is a figurative "baa", all they do is to pull down their figurative pants, and all they say is "Amen!"

.

FREEDOM OF EXPRESSION AND PROPAGANDA

05.04.2019

Let us begin with pathetic propaganda that only very well indoctrinated Western sheep-like humans can swallow: *Nicolás Maduro threatens to kill US troops in case of a US invasion of Venezuela* [1]!

What simplistic propaganda we find nowadays in Western mainstream media. Simplistic propaganda only for those who really have lost the ability to reason, isn't it?

First of all, why manipulate the reader's emotions with an intentionally and poorly chosen picture, showing an *upset* and *mad* Maduro, so that the (fallacious) idea of a *crazy man* can be injected into people's minds? Those that are supposedly right and are the owners of *absolute truth*, should not need to use such low blows, right?

Second: really? Do you want us to accept that, if the criminal US invades yet another country, we must blame the victim (Venezuela) and not the aggressor (USA), in case they kill enemy soldiers in their own land? Come on, if that happens, it will only be a natural consequence of the imperial aggression against Venezuela!

Yes, they will die! More the better! All of them, if possible! And it will not only be the Venezuelan military forces that will resist and kill the aggressors, but also an entire nation proud of its sovereignty, in love with its freedom, well informed and fully committed!

What the hell! How can "journalists" change the timeline of events like they just did here, voluntarily inverting the natural order of (criminal) action first and then (legitimate) reaction? This was just another dishonest attempt to create one more simplistic and fallacious reason to denigrate Maduro! And the most absurd part of this story is: westerners buy it!

Dear not dear Western "journalists", why don't you try to do the same about World War II and start blaming half of Europe for having killed the Nazi invaders?

Why don't you try to do the same and blame Vietnam or Laos for having been savagely destroyed and slaughtered by the United States?

Why don't you try to blame Africans for having been enslaved, traded and killed by the Portuguese or the British?

*

More propaganda. What can we say about the cheap silly propaganda produced by those who have lost the ability to reason and dare to call "dictatorship" one of the most democratic nations on Earth? And that dare to disrespect the democratic electoral process (read: popular will)? And that don't know how to add and subtract two-digit numbers? There's no need to say more, just look at the figures (being aware that the Venezuelan elections are among the ones that systematically receive the highest numbers of accredited international observers, including many from the US and the EU, whose observations have never detected any serious problem):

Source 2 - Comparison of elections' turn out in several countries

More propaganda. Look at what Western MSM produce to deceive the minds of those who also have lost the ability to reason and became submissive jellyfish-like humans. Look at the despicable AFP (a French "news agency", a propaganda tool based in the French Terrorist State; yes terrorist, because it terrorizes millions in Africa, in the Middle East and in the rest of the world; and do not ask me to be politically correct because this very same French Terrorist State *mistakenly* uses the same term to denigrate Iran or Syria!), also producing ignoble anti-Venezuela propaganda. Do these AFP journalistic *vampires* think that Venezuela has no right to protect its borders from Western Terrorism? Would they write such nonsense if the same were happening at a French border?

Source 3 – Sensationalist fake news produced by AFP to criticize Maduro's government

Seriously, what does AFP know about civil engineering or bridge construction? How do they know the bridge can't handle three or four containers full of sand? Have they done the maths? I don't think so. And the Western readers, do they swallow this pathetic and dishonest piece of propaganda? What if there were 20 trucks crossing the bridge carrying 20 containers full of sand, in a Venezuela under a

45

Yankee-Guaidó dictatorship, would the same bridge be able to handle it? Probably yes, but not 4 containers, if these 4 containers are there, under Maduro's government, to prevent the occurrence of further crimes against public property.

And why does AFP write about the reaction (blocking the bridge) and not about the Western-sponsored criminal actions that have taken place recently and are so well documented in Chapter 4 of this book?
The answer is obvious: because they are wrong; and those who are wrong, usually, they deceive, they do everything they can to deceive others. They divert the attention of the public, they distort reality, they lie, they cheat, they manipulate, etc.

More propaganda. More shameful, vile, unscrupulous propaganda. Propaganda in the form of recycled images from other conflicts and countries, later published as supposed pieces of evidence of crimes supposedly committed by the Venezuelan armed forces, the very same kind of shameful manipulation made against Syria during the last 8 years.

This trash-journalism helps to prove 2 points at once: first, Western Media do not feel ashamed to tell flagrant lies; second, if it is necessary to forge pieces of evidence against Venezuela in a country where there are hundreds of private anti-government media and where dozens of Western MSM interfere and attack the local government, one is lead to conclude that they can't find any true evidence of crimes committed by the government forces, that is to say, no evidence the Venezuelan government is oppressing or repressing its people:

Sources 4, 5, 6, 7 - 4 examples of forged pieces of evidence against Venezuela

You kind find more examples in this article published by Venezuelanalysis: *Constructing "Venezuela" Protests: a Photo Gallery* [8].

More propaganda. Extremely poor people "picking through trash for food" is something everyone can easily find in the streets of Lisbon, Jakarta or Bangkok, and the same is true in the USA, all countries that do not suffer embargoes, imagine if they did! Yet, manipulative journalism shows Venezuelans "picking through trash for food"[9] as evidence of failed socialism in Venezuela...

It's much more common to find this level of poverty in capitalist countries or vassal states of capitalist countries than in socialist states, the reason why a reasoning mind can easily conclude that the tweet above is a perfect example of a malicious and misleading Western (dis)information.

For instance, with a little bit of honesty, they could easily find poverty in the supposedly rich nation of Canada:

Source 10 – Evidence of poverty in Canada

Another type of propaganda is to talk about millions of Venezuelans fleeing to Colombia. Nonsense! Just search about real numbers and surprise yourself: you have been fed with a naked lie. The best (worst) Western Lying Media like Reuters can do is to predict chaos and horror in Venezuela: Four million Venezuelans may live in Colombia by 2021: minister[11]. Sure, 4 million, or even more, may leave Venezuela if US rapes and totally destroys Venezuela with total embargo and tomahawks. So what? Just more of the same US terrorism! Nothing else!

Another type of lack of freedom of speech is when one is not being allowed to say that many are fleeing the Yankee drug wars in Colombia and going to Venezuela. Don't CNN or BBC know it? How come? Haven't they heard about an international organization called the UN? The UN has the figures; Western sheep-like humans only lack the will to know those figures.

Source 12 – Data on the number of Colombian emigrants in Venezuela

*

Another kind of bullshit propaganda against Venezuela is to "report" the most absurd examples of nonsense, without providing any sources, in order to supposedly "protect the sources". But there's so much evidence of child soldiers fighting in so many conflicts, armed and supported by the West... why do they make up a false example of child soldiers supposedly forced to fight in Venezuela?

Source 13 – Reported nonsense

An expert on reporting absurd nonsense about Venezuela or Cuba is the US senator named Marco Rubio, always ready to lie in order to protect the interests of US Imperialism in general and the interests of the Miami *mafia* in particular.

Source 14 – Marco Rubio lying

Let's expose the grotesque lies of this liar.
First, Trump doesn't care about Venezuela. What he wants is to steal its oil, gold, and diamonds. And, as always, to destroy successful socialism to then say he proved that "socialism always fails". We, the West, should be tired of this criminal recipe... but, apparently no, not yet.

Second, there is no mass emigration from Venezuela to Colombia, and if there were, it would be the fault of the last seven consecutive years of Western economic war against Venezuela. To prove it, we have all the official indicators demonstrating the Bolivarian Venezuela to be an exceptional example of a society able to improve the standards of living for all human beings living inside its borders (read: *The Chávez Administration at 10 Years: The Economy and Social Indicators* [15] and *Venezuela cumple las Metas del Milenio 2010* [16]). To prove how guilty is the West of most economic problems Venezuela is suffering, there's an immense amount of serious investigative work (links to part of it can be found in the article *Venezuela for dummies* [17]). I would definitely recommend you to read the book *The visible hand of the market - Economic warfare in Venezuela (2012-2016)* [18].

Third, Colombia and the US are not "key" countries in the fight against drugs, but rather key countries in its production and proliferation. There's no shortage of evidence about it, but drug trafficking is not the subject of this essay. Venezuela smuggling drugs into the US, really? Ok, sure, tell me how, where, when, done by who? The proofs, please! Lying is easy. Accusing is easy. And the situation is particularly hilarious when the one accusing Venezuela of smuggling drugs into the US is a member of the Cuban *community* in Miami and a candidate to rule the US, the very same country that profits the most from the heroin produced in Afghanistan and the cocaine produced in Colombia or Peru! What an imbecile this Marco Rubio. And imagine how dumb must a *Western sheep-like human* be to swallow all these pathetic lies!

Fourth, "our hemisphere"? Really? Look how imperialism comes out of his mouth, so openly, so naturally! And the lobotomized Westerns don't even notice it!

What "our hemisphere"? Your "Imperial USA" has a seat at the UN, not your "hemisphere".

In that hemisphere, there are dozens of countries that, according to the United Nations Charter, are supposed to be independent and sovereign! What a fool this Rubio is!

Oh, really, Maduro is supposedly asking Russia to establish (legal) bases in his country. Sure. So what? Where's the problem? Doesn't my homeland (Portugal) host several Yankee military bases? Doesn't the US have more than 800 bases in at least 144 countries? Isn't the US building new military bases in Colombia?

Come on, the US has numerous illegal military bases occupying countries such as Cuba or Syria! But for the Western sheep-like humans, somehow, everything is *just fine*! Come on, how come Western human beings fail to detect such obvious incoherencies? Such blatant double standards?

Fifth, Hezbollah in Venezuela is a lie unless Rubio can prove it's true. Good Luck. But, if it were true, what would be the problem of having Maduro giving "operating space to Hezbollah" (a Lebanese Party with several seats at the Lebanese Parliament)? And what's the problem of having Venezuela hosting troops from its ally Iran? A really dangerous problem would be to have the US invading Venezuela and building colonial military bases like the ones they shamelessly built in Afghanistan, in Syria or in Iraq. Come on, how can Western sheep-like humans not notice such glaring incoherence?

Last two examples of ridiculous Western propaganda about nonexistent "conflicts" at the border mixed with plenty of Western interventionism, and unauthorized use of the Red Cross logo to disguise terrorism and interventionism as "humanitarian aid":

Source 19 - Unauthorized use of the Red Cross logo

Available footage shows us the "opposition" vandalizing and burning everything they can find, with unnecessary use of extreme violence, throwing Molotov cocktails, etc. Instead of calling it vandalism and extreme violence, Western Lying Media prefer to lie and call it *oppression of peaceful protesters by the evil regime*:

Source 20 - Lies of colonial media

When facing such obvious evidence of Western Lying Media lying, I wonder: are Westerners still able to reason? To think logically? Can we still find some reasoning minds in the West? Sure we can, but only a few, a tiny minority. A tiny minority of marginalized voiceless beings lost in that Orwellian dictatorship of imposed consensuses and of institutionalized *truths*. No, I'm not talking about North Korea, I am talking about Europe and North America.

The others, the immense majority of westerners, they blindly and submissively swallow the most pathetic and grotesque lies. For instance, some weeks ago RTP, a Portuguese television channel, reported a gross lie affirming (without any proof, since it's a gross lie) that the Venezuelan government "closed several Venezuelan private media"! Unbelievable. And what did Portuguese sheep-like humans do? They baaed and then they said "amen".

If you make part of the first group, if you honor the truth and if your brain is still functioning properly, please read essays like this one: *Venezuela in the middle of a media war, a prelude to a plain war?* [21]

If you make part of the second group, I believe you are a lost cause. But I hope you can prove me wrong. I really do!

*

Freedom of speech, right. Let's talk about freedom of speech.

Where is Western freedom of expression when the West prevents socialist and pro-Maduro South American countries (Cuba, Bolivia, Nicaragua, etc.) from expressing themselves in international forums convened by the US and its vassals? Call it Orwellian consensus, instead!

Where is freedom of expression in the United States, if people go to jail for expressing support for Maduro's government?

Source 22 – US citizens arrested while protesting in favor of Maduro's government

Where is the freedom of expression in the United States when a Canadian journalist defending the truth about Venezuela is prevented from entering US territory?

Source 23 - Canadian journalist prevented from entering US territory

Where is Western freedom of expression when thousands of people and/or organizations supporting Maduro's government are completely censured? Yes, Twitter itself (an US corporation, directly interfering with Venezuela's politics) admits to have erased[24] accounts of people and/or organizations that, according to the official statement of this Yankee corporation (which spies on us and delivers our private data hand in hand to its criminal government), supposedly "appear to be engaged in a state-backed influence campaign targeting domestic audiences" or were engaged in a *"state-backed influence campaign"*.

What do this Orwellian accusations mean? Is Twitter arguing that Venezuelans have no right to tweet their support for the Venezuelan government? Can't Venezuelan citizens have links to the Venezuelan government? What is wrong with that? In the US, there are millions of citizens with all sort of links to the two criminal organizations called Democratic Party and Republican Party. Twitter doesn't seem to be worried about it. Furthermore, Venezuela is an independent nation; any measure Twitter takes to censor pro-government Venezuelans and influence the levels of popular support qualifies as foreign intervention in the internal affairs of a sovereign state. Shame on Twitter!

Source 25 – Twitter took down 2,000 accounts located in Venezuela

*

Censorship, right. Let's also talk about censorship.

What do you have to say, dear reader, to the fact that Venezuelan Telesur and Russian RT were prevented from following the Lima Group's meeting (about intervening and interfering in Venezuela) in Canada? Come on Western "free world", where's your loudly proclaimed "free world"? What have you done with the *Munich Declaration of the Duties and Rights of Journalists* [26]? Where are the United Nations Charter and the International Law you helped writing and creating?

You can't explain it, can you? After all, the censors are those who call themselves "democratic" and "free", and who wrongly accuse the Venezuelan government of "censoring" local media. Whoops, what a mess, right? For more information on this issue, read *Russian and alternative media denied access to Venezuela meeting in Canada* [27].

Seriously, look how the Government of Canada responded to Venezuelan Telesur's request[28]:

"Thank you for your interest in the 10th ministerial meeting of Lima Group in Ottawa. This email is to let you know have NOT been accredited as media."

No explanation whatsoever! Amazing and inexistent Canadian freedom of expression!

Then let the West tell us myths and tales about censorship in Venezuela, when the West censors a Venezuelan state media and prevents it from following and reporting a meeting where Western states and their South American client states were going to discuss their plan to force a coup d'état in the very same Venezuela!

And Western sheep-like humans swallow this? Really? Wow, you Western sheep-like humans, you swallow all these contradictions without noticing anything wrong? Really? Don't you notice here a fundamental contradiction? A grotesque lack of logic and lack of seriousness? Don't you see how unscrupulous are the Western Lying Media? Come on...

I insist, where is Western freedom of expression when the West censors a Cuban newspaper's article about Venezuela that was shared on Facebook?

Where is freedom of expression when the West censors numerous YouTube videos, Facebook publications and tweets that do not fit in with the Western rhetoric and that provide plenty of evidence of Western terrorism in Syria, Libya, Venezuela and throughout the whole world?

Check these articles of mine and see how much content has been deleted (censored) by YouTube (Google), Facebook and Twitter (3 U.S. corporations):

- White Helmets, humanists or terrorists?[31]
- Extermínio nuclear, sim por favor![32] (in Portuguese)
- O quão a Amnistia Internacional adora o terrorismo na Síria[33] (in Portuguese)
- A RTP, SIC, TVI, CMTV e companhia são apoiantes do terrorismo na Síria![34] (in Portuguese)
- And many others.

To learn more about the tactics and excuses used to censor dissent, please read the three articles I wrote about the unstoppable censorship on Facebook:

- Censorship on Facebook[35]
- Fuck Facebook, fuck Zuckerberg[36]
- Orwellian Facebook[37]

And here is one more evidence that Facebook went mad, grossly censoring everything and everyone who dares to resist, including my Facebook page for this website Nomadic Thoughts. In January, this page of mine, with more than 5500 followers, suddenly, without any notification, was deleted by Facebook. If you don't believe me, check it:

Source 38 - My Facebook page censored

Just a few days ago, Twitter suspended the account of a Venezuelan I used to follow. Please check what a Twitter account looks like after Twitter's decision to censor it:

Source 39 - Venezuelan account suspended by Twitter

Do you want more examples of alternative media being censored or attacked by Western *freedom of speech*? Check how Western Puppet Guaidó and his fellow coup plotters call for the censorship of alternative Venezuelan media like Venezuelanalysis[40]:

Source 41 – Document published by the faked Guaidó's Embassy to the OAS

Poor coup plotters, they go wild when confronted with facts and arguments! *Our* Portuguese grandparents, who taught us that "those who are right, shall not fear anything" were far wiser than the overwhelming majority of modern-day *Portuguese sheep-like humans*.

In a true democracy, even if you lie, you shouldn't be censored. The US loves to brag about its First Amendment[42], about "freedom of expression" and other "freedoms". So why don't they stand up for the very same principles in Venezuela? And why does the US support this Guaidó who calls for the censorship of those who disagree with him and of those who endlessly expose the crimes of the terrorist "opposition" of which Guaidó himself is a member?

This crazy traitor named Guaidó really *reasons* as a true dictator. Did you read it? Guaidó demands the media call him "president", while Maduro must be mentioned as the "self-proclaimed President" of Venezuela! Seriously?

And *Western sheep-like humans swallow* this guy? Amazing.

*

Twitter/Facebook/Western bullshit "freedom of speech" is implemented through the elimination of accounts owned by Venezuelans and foreigners supporting Venezuela? Really?

Come on dear westerners, in democracy, can we have or not different opinions?

In real democracies like Russia or Venezuela, yes, people are allowed to have different opinions. But, apparently, in Europe and in the US, people are no longer allowed to express different opinions. In the West, only official absolute truths are allowed; only Orwellian consensuses are allowed. White is black, ignorance is strength and, very well trained citizens, when listening anti-Venezuela or anti-Syria propaganda, they obediently answer with a cute "baa"!

Yes, Orwellian absolute truths. Yes, a dystopian consensus. Because everything else is censored, blocked and erased so that the Western sheep neither sees nor knows anything. Then please tell me stories about North Korea, while I fall asleep. European and Yankees are so mentally tortured, with this powerful and effective Orwellian imposition of consensuses, that they end up believing North Koreans are the brainwashed ones and not themselves!

And by the way, the consensual idea westerners have about "North Korea being a land of brainwashed Koreans victims of government-imposed consensuses" is a perfect example of the many Orwellian consensuses reigning in the West, don't you think? Western *North-Korean-like* consensus about North Korea, the kind of consensus we probably will not be able to find even in North Korea! How ironic, no?
Westerners believe everybody thinks the same in North Korea and submissively swallow everything the North Korean "regime" imposes... well, if that's true, we could arrange a perfect marriage between Westerners and North Koreans!

And by the way, between Europeans and Thais! Yes, I'm 100% sure about it! The Thai regime imposes or tries to impose absurd consensuses over every single aspect of life in Thailand! Yet, westerners love Thailand as a tourist destination and, therefore, self-impose reality filters in order to not see what happens in Thailand. For China, the same westerners use some sort of augmented reality gadgets that make them see inexistent problems of the same kind of the existing problems they pretend not to see in Thailand. Yes, *poor neurotic West!*

*

Speaking of Thailand, where I live at the moment, do you want me to tell you a sad joke about freedom of speech?

Some weeks ago I met a Polish couple (yes, from Poland, that 51st U.S. state called Poland) complaining that their daughter could not receive the last edition of The Economist (give me a second, I'm going to metaphorically vomit, I will be right back) here in Thailand, due to its "sensitive content", according to the non-elected authorities that have been governing Thailand for the last 5 years.

Because they were Polish, coming from that country of anti-socialist and anti-communist fundamentalism, of rising fascism, of unfounded Russophobia and of fans of US/EU/NATO imperial terrorism, I couldn't let it pass. I immediately framed them with their own Western incoherencies.

I asked them, convincingly: "So, explain me this: in Venezuela, a gangster named Guaidó, supported by the US, who was not even a presidential candidate, proclaimed himself the "President of Venezuela"; now he dares walking on the streets of Venezuela without fear of being arrested; he dares to give interviews to hundreds of journalists working for Venezuelan anti-government private media that were supposed to be censored by Maduro's "oppressive regime"; and the West calls all this "dictatorship", "regime", "oppression", "lack of freedom" of expression?"

Source 43 - Juan Guaidó surrounded by journalists in Venezuela

56

I continued: "On the other hand, in this 'democratic' regime of unelected Thai rulers, where we can find plenty of military bases[44] controlled by their US masters, a dysfunctional and dystopian nation constantly romanticized in the West as the "Land of Smile", here, in this so-called "paradise", your daughter cannot receive the last edition of a North American propaganda tool named The Economist?"

And finally, I said: "If what you told me is true, and I believe it is, can you please explain to me why the Western MSM constantly mention nonexistent 'censorship in Venezuela', while they never mention the obvious censorship that truly takes place every day in Thailand?"

The Polish man, after he and his wife having insisted on a long and awkward silence, looked at the fruit basket on the table and literally said: "Let's change the subject, let's talk about mangoes". No joke. He really said so! This real-life anecdote perfectly illustrates what I dare to call Western sheep-like humans, Western jellyfish-like humans or Western zombies! Yes, I know what I have been writing in this book sounds extremely rude, but it is not my intention to be or sound rude. I'm just pragmatically describing Western reality as I perceive it. *Mea culpa*!

Finally, and because we were talking about that fundamentalist propaganda tool that goes by the name of The Economist, and talking about Venezuela, look at the pro-Guaidó cover and content of their Twitter account[45]: The Economist illustrating parallelism between Juan Guaidó and the Statue of Liberty? Give me a break!

*

Let's now talk about Western's nemesis: Russia.

The Western media in general and the French, in particular, keep calling RT a deceitful tool of Kremlin's propaganda. The only problem is that RT broadcasts shows like CrossTalk in which people with absolutely opposing views can debate live for long periods of time! Live! Tell me which French or other Western media outlets propose a live debate between a pro-Assad and an anti-Assad, or between an anti-Maduro and a pro-Maduro, or an anti-China and a pro-China, or a communist and a soulless neoliberal? You can't find it, right? And do you know why you can't? Because there's no such thing in France, there's no such thing in Portugal. In Russia yes. In Europe no.

Source 46 - Paradigm Shift: Debate at SPIEF 2019 with Peter Lavelle

I myself disagree with much of what Peter Lavelle (the host of this show, a North American right-wing conservative) says, but I admire him for inviting communists, anarchists or neoliberals, atheists or religious fanatics, Iranians or North Americans! Bravo! There's nothing like this in *my* "democratic" Portugal! There's nothing like this in *my* arrogant Europe!

And it is not only Crosstalk, but we can also find the same reasonable and fair approach in most of the shows RT has to offer. All kinds of opinions, proposing opposite and even contradicting perspectives, are voiced on RT, often live (unlike BBC or CNN). For instance, watch Eva Bartlett debating or trying to debate with a supporter of terrorism in Syria, live on RT:

Source 47 - Journalists face off over Syria news sources in RT debate

No, the Russian RT is not like the Yankee CNN of constant interruptions when it is not acceptable (for CNN and the Empire) to have inconvenient truths being said live:

Source 48 - CNN "Technical Difficulties" and Censorship

So many "technical failures" on CNN, so few or even nonexistent on RT. Are CNN and the Yankees technologically backward, and RT and Russians technologically more advanced or, are CNN and Yankees fans of censorship, and RT and Russians truth supporters of freedom of expression? Or both?

Yet, how many times do I read *Portuguese sheep-like humans* complaining that I "don't use credible sources like CNN or BBC on my essays and articles"? And I'm sure these *sheep-like humans* do believe CNN and BBC are credible sources and RT is not.

The systematic and desired production and propagation of lies by CNN and BBC is very well documented and there are brave journalists who have no problems to expose and prove it, as John Pilger did in his brilliant documentary *The War You Don't See* [49]. My dear Portuguese critics proposing me CNN and BBC as "credible sources", apparently, never noticed what Pilger already documented.

But I do notice. And I ask them to show me a journalist, just one, just a single journalist, working for a Western news outlet, as hyper-critical and hyper-rational and supporting everything he/she says with plenty of data, as the brilliant Russian journalist Murad Gazdiev does? Seriously, show me just one Gazdiev-like journalist working for Western mainstream media.

In the meantime, I propose you to watch an example of Gazdiev's hyper-critical and hyper-rational reports:

Source 50 - Now Maduro's Turn: US labels Venezuelan leader 'dictator' same as Assad, Hussein, Gaddafi

And for those who insist that there's no freedom of expression in Russia, I invite all of them to explain how RT, a supposed propaganda tool ruled by Mr. Putin, invited the hysterical progressive *Barbie* named Ksenia Sobchak to be interviewed live on TV. I remind you that Ksenia Sobchak, at the time a candidate for the upcoming Russian presidential elections, is an outspoken supporter of Navalni, known in the Western Lying Media as a "political prisoner". Yet, she spoke for more than half an hour on the very same RT ("funded by the Kremlin"), firing insults at Russia and Putin, and violently disrespecting the journalist interviewing her! Could someone in the West explain to me this very strange phenomenon?

Source 51 - Candidate against all: Ksenia Sobchak

RT employs some of the best and brightest English-speaking journalists who cannot find work in the US, UK or Australia because they dare to be fiercely independent and critical of the West and its client states. A perfect example is the American Lee Camp and his show Redact Tonight, who openly complains that nobody would let him work for Western news channels:

Many in the West, and specifically in the US, criticize their fellow citizens like Lee Camp "working for the enemy" (read, "Russian RT"). But they fail to acknowledge the most basic facts: US MSM have all the money and power and audience to hire Lee Camp or to convince him to work for them. Actually, Lee Camp said so in an interview. He said he would be glad to work for MSM in his own country! But he can't! He can't because he wouldn't be allowed to say what he thinks and, worse, he wouldn't be allowed to tell the truths he is aware of.

If Western MSM can't stand watching Western journalists working for RT, the solution is simple and easy! Let Lee Camp or Abby Martin express themselves freely on their own media outlets, and they will surely accept to earn more money to expose the exact same inconvenient truths!

The problem is not RT dear westerners. The problem is that Western journalists are prevented from working as journalists in the West, so they seek refuge on RT. If Western MSM really wanted to destroy RT (by stealing their best journalists), they could do it very easily.

Yet, the Western MSM continue to do the very opposite.

*

For instance, Western media shamelessly, even proudly, took part in the making up of chemical attacks in Syria (Ghouta 2013, Khan Shaykhun 2016, Ghouta 2018), to then support criminal missile attacks on Syria delivered by terrorist nations like France, the UK, the US, and Israel.

In 2018, RT visited Ghouta and interviewed witnesses and victims of the alleged chemical attack. RT proved the whole chemical attack scam to be a big laughable lie. Then the Russian government brought the witnesses to The Hague. And again, the Western media accused RT and Russia of being nothing but a bunch of liars and propagandists. Sure!

Now, one year later, Riam Dalati, a journalist working for BBC finally admitted that there was no chemical attack in Douma and that it had all been staged[53]!

But RT produces propaganda, right?

Source 54 - Douma chemical attack video was staged - BBC Syria producer

On March 13, 2018, for many hours, and thanks to RT and Ruptly *livestreams*, I watched live the last Syrian civilians leaving Ghouta hugging and kissing their liberators: the Syrian Arab Army (SAA). I was in Portugal. I was in Braga, in that Portuguese land of obscurantism and religious fanaticism, but also the land of new technologies, where there's a quite fast internet. And, where there's internet, one can watch RT and Ruptly *livestreams*. But people don't. Portuguese sheep-like humans and their fellow European sheep-like humans watch Western propaganda and only Western propaganda.

I usually watch both, so I can compare them. And, on that day, I did watch both, simultaneously. While the Portuguese professional streetwalkers working for RTP, SIC and TVI were talking about the "final massacre", about the SAA committing "one more genocide" and creating a "giant open-air cemetery in Ghouta", I was watching live a careful and peaceful SAA operation during which thousands of civilians were liberated. I watched the very same civilians and the very same soldiers hugging each other and crying together[55]!

Sources 56, 57, 58 – Footage disproving Western MSM lies on Ghouta

But RT is the one producing propaganda, right dear brainwashed Portuguese people?

I could spend the rest of the day here writing down facts proving how RT is infinitely more impartial, more objective and more serious than all the propagandistic Western Lying Media combined. But I have done it so many times, just read the many articles I have written on the subject.

The important now is to say that this very same RT is being violently and madly attacked by the shameless French media, the French

61

media who lie every single day, who have always lied, who have always supported and fostered the most atrocious crimes against humanity. Those same French media that are now offering this kind of outrageous and Orwellian campaigns against RT:

Source 59 – Anti-Putin propaganda in French television

Yes, dear reader, simplistic, primitive, grotesque, pathetic, childish anti-RT propaganda on French television! And the worst is that the target audience, I'm not kidding, the target audience is the French children! Yes, you read it well! French children!

I wonder what kind of reaction would George Orwell have while watching this Orwellian stuff. I actually don't know what to say, this is too serious and appalling! Even the word "Orwellian" is not strong enough to describe what is going on in France right now! Please read RT's article on the subject and amaze yourself, amaze yourself *ad infinitum*: *'Putin – tsar of disinfo': French TV teaches children about 'Russian fake news'* [60].

Seriously, what's the purpose of this France 4 show? To help children (who don't give a shit about geopolitics) recognize fake "fake news" supposedly produced by the *demonic* "Russian propagandists"! And how do they do that? They do it by producing fake news about Russia, Putin and RT, viciously manipulating words and phrases they find on RT, blatantly offering dishonest propaganda against RT, Russia, and the Russians. Shame on you France 4! Shame on you French Public Service.

Bravo, French propaganda, bravo! Let's all applaud this chic and fancy Gaulish crap!

Is it possible to create something more intellectually disturbing than this, in the realm of propaganda? Personally, I think France, with this televised circus, reached and even surpassed the very top of what reasonable people call "Orwellian propaganda". This circus is no doubt worse than other abusive Orwellianisms like the North American Snopes[61] or the French Décodex[62], two fake fact-checking sites hunting for fake "fake news" allegedly produced by media outlets in non-submissive countries like Russia, Venezuela, Iran or China.

*

Source 63 – Screenshot of a tweet

As you can confirm by reading the content of the screenshot above, Twitter said it "can't show you everything", so it "automatically hides photos that might contain sensitive content". Perhaps fair if it were true, but it is not true. There's absolutely no sensitive content in that tweet. Check it by yourself:

Source 64 - Same tweet when opened

The "sensitive content" is an official document published by the Canadian administration. It states that the Canadian government decided to censor Venezuelan Telesur, preventing it from covering the Lima Group Summit in Canada! Scandalous Canadian behavior, yes, for sure. But not sensitive!

Sensitive what, the Canadian speech? The Canadian flag? Their publicly known email account?

Give me a break. This is a perfect example to illustrate the subject of the very same article containing the tweet that was censored: the lack of freedom of expression and the abundance of propaganda in the West!

Because no, there's nothing sensitive in that tweet, unless the shameful factual truth of Telesur (run by the Venezuelan government) being censored by the Canadian government is too "sensitive" for Twitter! Twitter had no choice but to censor a tweet about Canada censoring Venezuelan Telesur, right? I see your point, Twitter.

And life goes on. And zombie-like westerners will continue to believe the West has freedom of speech. And Western sheep-like humans will continue to believe there's censorship in Venezuela.

What about freedom of expression in Brazil? Do you want to talk about attacks on freedom of expression and propaganda in Brazil, committed by its fascist President Bolsonaro? We'd be here all day!

In Brazil, fascist Bolsonaro openly says, live on TV, that he will end with the funding of arts and culture because those social institutions are "leftist" and "bring dangerous ideas". Check what Jair Bolsonaro is doing in Brazil and then think about it, carefully, dear not dear Western sheep-like humans, think about it.

Then think about the false accusations you pronounce against Maduro. Westerners accuse Maduro of what he doesn't do but are not capable of criticizing Bolsonaro for what he actually does and openly proposes to do.

Source 65 - Fascism in Brazil

*

What about freedom of expression in the West, where its very pro-imperialist Atlantic Council is now also acting as guardian of the *truth*, as caretaker of Western newspeak[66]?

Source 67 - Facebook censorship conducted in line with "Integrity Initiative" aims

*

What about freedom of expression in the United States where a journalist is fired by CNN after telling inconvenient truths about Israeli apartheid that oppresses and humiliates millions of Palestinians?

Source 68 - CNN commentator Marc Lamont Hill fired for this pro-Palestine speech

What about the United States, where an Iranian-American journalist, an employee of Iranian PressTV, is indefinitely detained, without any charge, without any explanation?

Read, on the subject, *Trump's Anti-Iran Campaign & NDAA Clause Behind 'Inhumane' Detention of PressTV Anchor Marzieh Hashemi* [71].

What about the US, where officials want to ban their own citizens from campaigning for the boycott of goods produced by the terrorist state of Israel (despite its First Amendment)?

Source 72 - Will boycotting Israel become illegal?

For Western governments, everything is allowed! For Venezuelan coup-plotters hand-picked and supported by the U.S., everything is allowed. For Western Lying Media everything is allowed. And the Western sheep-like humans say "baa"!

Then, Venezuela is accused of being what it is not, and Western sheep-like humans clap their hands to all the bullshit pronounced and even swallow it! And many of them adore the US and the democracy and the freedom of speech the US does not have! And, I insist, they are mad at Maduro for what he is not and for what he does not do! Holy innocence! Holy ignorance! Holy stupidity!

*

And to speak of freedom of expression, propaganda and Venezuela altogether, what about the Venezuelan private media that openly participated in the 2002 coup d'état, those media that knew in advance what was going to happen, how and when, by who, and participated directly and actively in the implementation of the 48 hours coup?

Yes, many of them were amnestied by Chávez. In the U.S., they would be locked up for good. Calling for the death of the head of state live on TV, offending, calling for violence and unconstitutional measures... Try, dear reader, please try to do it in your home country and then tell me how *funny* it was!

Watch *The War on Democracy* [73] and *The Revolution Will Not be Televised* [74] to confirm what I just wrote, how the media participated, yes, actively participated in the 2002 coup, reporting deaths before they happened (which implies, at the least, complicity). Later, thanks to serious investigations, we learned the criminal snipers who killed civilians were foreign mercenaries (read the book *Abril golpe Adentro* [75] and watch the documentary *Llaguno Bridge - Keys to a Massacre*[76]).

These TV channels like Globovision and these newspapers like El Nacional, they are still open and operating and supporting more coups and more economic terrorism! All this in a country where the Portuguese RTP said, a few weeks ago, that the government is shutting down private media! Can you imagine? Yes, you can. You have already heard the same from the Lying Media also lying in your country! For RTP and other Western Lying Media, black is white, war is peace and the sky is green!

Please read the book *Dictatura Mediática en Venezuela - Investigación de unos medios por encima de toda sospecha* [77], by Luis Britto García, or *Psicoterrorismo Mediático, La Disociación Sicótica* [78], by Erick Rodríguez Miérez, to understand how this whole game of manipulation works in the case of Venezuela and it gets away with total impunity. Read books like *La guerra mediática contra Venezuela*[79] to realize how distorted and manipulated the Venezuelan reality is by vile Western Lying Media such as the pseudo-leftist El País in Spain.

In Venezuela, there are more than 100 private TV channels, hundreds of private newspapers and magazines, all property of oligarchs who participate in the economic destruction of their country and who illegally call for crimes against their nation. And nobody shuts them down! And their billionaire owners walk free in the streets of Caracas (or rather Miami)!

In Venezuela, there are a few public TV channels, such as VTV. Guaidó and his companions already called for the closure of VTV, proving they fear the truths VTV spreads. Carmona, the President that lasted 48 hours back in 2002, did the same. What else must be said and shown to make Westerners open their eyes, hear and acknowledge the obvious and real reality?

Venezuela has what no other nation on Earth has for real: communitarian media. Communitarian media are state-funded media (infrastructure, equipment, etc.) made available to the people, to the members of the community, to the communities, to anyone who wants and has information to share. The state pays for it, finances it, but does not control it. The people (willing to take part) control them. They are neither produced by private corporations nor by the state, they are produced by the people!

Is there in the world a better example of freedom of expression than this one? I'm sure there's not. Prove me wrong... or shut up.

And yet, over and over again, these community media are attacked, vandalized and burned by the terrorist "opposition"! Public property, expensive, very expensive, made available for those who want to express themselves freely. All this destroyed by the very same people who accuse Maduro of being a dictator, by the very same people who claim to be defenders of freedom! Come on, time to wake up, no?

And for *god* sake, why dear reader, why, for what reason we never see Western journalists "crying" for the crimes committed against their fellow journalists working in Venezuelan communitarian media?

I tell you why. They don't cry for these crimes against communitarian journalism for the same reason they don't cry for Julian Assange. Western journalists cry for Khashoggi but not for Julian Assange because those Western journalists are not journalists. They are professional streetwalkers who sold their souls to the devil (read "International Economic Dictatorship"). They only care about money, not journalism, not information, not justice, not the truth. And the few honest and true journalists in the West, psychologically incapable of prostituting themselves, well, they simply can't work for Western media.

Yet, the Western populace, the Western sheep-like humans, the Western zombies, they don't know any of this. There's no excuse, but it is true. Westerners don't know any of this.

And, by the way, where are the Portuguese communitarian media where I (and others like me) could publish this very same work you are reading now?

*

To finish this chapter, and because Western sheep-like humans seem to be so "interested" in elections being held in undemocratic states, let's talk about... let me see... the magnificent examples of Indonesia and Thailand! Where are the reports on the fake and undemocratic elections recently held in Indonesia and Thailand?

I checked Portuguese and other Western media and I found almost nothing about it, and not a single critic about the clearly undemocratic procedures! Even if the Western media's accusations against the Venezuelan government were to be true, for a matter of coherence, the Western media constantly attacking the Venezuelan government for what it doesn't do, should definitely do the same for what Thai and Indonesian governments clearly do. Where there's no consistency, there's no credibility.

Otherwise, how can Western media and Western audiences miss that in Indonesia (where millions of communists, atheists, and Chinese people were killed after the US-sponsored coup d'état in 1965), in that astonishing "democracy", it is illegal to be a communist or an atheist?

Indonesia, where there are anti-communist museums.

Indonesia, where truly left-wing parties cannot participate in elections.

Indonesia, where the very "democratic" local authorities burned left-wing literature in public squares, right before the recent elections.

Nothing, absolutely nothing in Western MSM truly exposing the crimes committed in Indonesia or in Thailand against the freedom of expression and against those who dare to participate in some sort of elections.

The Western journalists can even go wild, losing their minds accusing Venezuela of being an oppressive dictatorship, but nothing comes out of their mouths about the Indonesian genocide in Papua. Nothing about the destruction of books. Nothing about political parties prevented from participating in elections. Nothing about candidates being arrested before the elections. Absolutely nothing.

And the Western sheep-like humans still believe Western MSM tell them *the truth, the whole truth and nothing but the truth.* And they believe Western MSM never omit anything important.

As for Thailand, quote-unquote. Like Indonesia, Thailand is an undemocratic state. The last democratically elected government was overthrown by a military coup that resulted in horrible things I will not write here but are easy to find on the Internet.

In March 2019, a sort of election was finally held in Thailand. But the way the authorities in this country threatened certain candidates and sang certain songs in allusion to certain losses of lives in the past, at the hands of certain other authorities of the same nature, destroyed any credibility the recent elections might have had.

I am not saying, I am simply asking: Is there freedom of expression in Thailand?

Dear reader, if you do not know how to answer my question, here are some articles to start digging: *Cybersecurity bill passed* [80], *MCOT removes TV host over students' vote* [81], *NLA's cyber bill rush shows poor intent* [82], *Future Forward Party in 'fake news' brouhaha* [83].

If you want to search deeper, you should start following brave Thais like the one behind this Twitter account: BarbaricThais[84].

OPPRESSION AND REPRESSION

10.05.2019

It's amazing the amount of misinformation that has been produced in recent years about oppression and/or repression in Venezuela. I only ask Western journalists to explain to me what kind of "oppressive regime" allows the criminal opposition to commit all these outrageous acts of terror:

- 'Peaceful' opposition setting police vehicles on fire;[1]
- 'Peaceful' opposition attacking police forces with rockets;[2]
- Pro-government man shot dead and then set on fire by the 'peaceful' opposition;[3]
- 'Peaceful' protesters setting a young pro-government man on fire inside a shopping mall;[4]
- 'Peaceful' protesters burning and destroying the house of a humble government supporter;[5]
- 'Peaceful' protesters burning and destroying a public hospital;[6]
- 'Peaceful' protesters causing serious damage in 15 universities, including UNEFA.[7]

The examples are endless.

*

Tell me, what kind of repression are people suffering there if, after having done all this and far worse, those criminals in the opposition continue to walk free on the streets of Venezuela, doing more of the same and calling for more crimes on the hundreds of private-owned radios, newspapers, and TVs?

On the contrary, all these barbarian criminals, directly or indirectly paid by the War Empire (aka the USA) to the tune of dozens of millions of dollars, should be oppressed and repressed. Yes, they should, because they make the weakest and most vulnerable citizens suffer, and because they do all they can to destroy a living and successful example of socialism that actually does its best for the weakest and the most vulnerable! And, of course, because crimes are crimes!

Tell me what kind of oppression is that in which Guaidó, an agent of the illegal U.S. interference[8] in Venezuela, is allowed to walk free on the streets of his nation, calling for unconstitutional coups and illegal foreign military interventions while being interviewed by crowds of journalists working for anti-government private media:

Source 9 - Juan Guaidó surrounded by journalists in Venezuela

Tell me, what kind of oppression allows Guaidó to leave Venezuela and then go back to do all this without being arrested?

Tell me, what kind of oppression is the one which organizes elections? Three months ago, just a few days after the beginning of this recent Western aggression on Venezuela, Maduro's government proposed new parliamentary elections and, from what we could see[10], many Venezuelans were happy with the proposal.

*

I wonder: do the Western sheep-like humans know what real oppression and repression are?

Oppression was what they had in Venezuela before the Bolivarian revolution, as the Venezuelan people (the Bolivarian ones, Chavistas, pro-Maduro) reminded us a few weeks ago[11].

Watch and learn about Caracazo[12], the massacre of several thousand Venezuelans at the hands of the neoliberal regime, allied with the US. In 1989, the neoliberal regime was suffocating the Venezuelan people, economically, in such a way that an outburst of dissatisfied civilians was inevitable. Avoidable and highly reprehensible was the massacre of thousands of unarmed civilians but, because Venezuela was ruled by a US puppet, westerners didn't notice nor care about what happened.

Source 13 - Joel Linares on Venezuela's 1989 'Caracazo' Uprising Against Neoliberalism

Western sheep-like humans criticize Maduro for massacres he never committed. The criminal opposition does kill, but who in the West cares about their crimes? Nobody! Westerners don't even know about the massacre that took place in 1989! So, what's wrong with Western sheep-like humans?

Are they all living in a very big desert which existence I never noticed and where there's no access to books or the internet?

Or perhaps, as Vltchek asks: the *Western public does not know or does not want to know* [14]? The second option is probably the right one, but I would add something more. The title of this book: Westerners have lost the ability to reason!

*

Now, if you want to hear about real repression and not fictitious repression, let's talk about the US, of course. Because look, in a very incoherent way, westerners completely close their eyes to the most barbaric and horrible examples of violence committed in the US and its vassal states. On the other hand, they are always ready to talk about alleged "violence committed by the Venezuelan oppressive regime"! What an infinite incoherence! BBC, CNN, DW, France24 and their *brother in lies* have completely *boiled* westerners' brains!

Please check on YouTube how real repression looks like in the US. Look how US police forces injure and torture their fellow-citizens. Here's a list of proofs: *Raw Footage: Police Brutality Compilation* [15].

Do you want a more recent example? Well, there are so many over the internet! For instance, look how police officers in the US electrocuted the testicles of a man with a taser: *Man's testicles tasered during horrific police arrest* [16].

Has anyone ever seen images like these ones coming from Venezuela, Cuba, Eritrea or North Korea? No! And please, don't come again with Western fake news about North Korean leader throwing uncles and cousins into shark pools! Fool yourself if you want, but lies are lies, fake news is fake news, unproven allegations are unproven allegations, including the most ridiculous ones like *"15 state-approved hairstyles"*[17] or "there is no freedom of religion in North Korea"[18]!

If westerners are willing to search about real oppression and real repression, there's no shortage of real cases happening in the US. One must be honest and coherent when showing concern for the suffering of other human beings! Cherry-picking and picking fake cases is not a very humanistic approach!

And if westerners research about it, they will find plenty of grotesque data explaining why the US has reached such an advanced level of Orwellian dystopia where adults and children are arrested (sometimes indefinitely) in private prisons[19], and where the incarceration rates are absurdly high:

Source 20 – Top incarceration rate in the world (US ranked in first place)

*

Look at repression in France[21]!

France and oppression, almost two synonymous words nowadays.

In the streets of the French terrorist state (yes terrorist state, because it terrorizes millions in Syria, Libya, Ivory Coast, Mali, etc.), unarmed people, even children[22], are attacked by their very oppressive and repressive police forces! Yet, brainwashed westerners see no violence, no oppression, no repression, nothing, absolutely nothing wrong in France. In France, policemen do their job. That's all!

I invite you to read two articles of mine on this subject:

Overthrow the oppressive French regime! (PART 1)[23]
Overthrow the oppressive French regime! (PART 2)[24]

For the gullible Western rabble, oppression and repression are only when the Venezuelan police forces passively protect public property and borders, while being attacked with rockets, grenades, fire and Molotov cocktails.

But in France? Who cares about police forces cracking down on peaceful protesters! Who cares if France decides to oppress its people with laws outlawing the act of protesting, right?

Source 25 – French lawmakers approve anti-riot bill

*

Look at the grotesque oppression occurring in Saudi Arabia, an ally of the United States, where peaceful protesters are arrested, executed and beheaded, as happened in 2016 to Nimr al-Nimr[26] and other 46 Saudi Arabian Shia Muslims:

Source 27 - Saudi Arabia executes Shi'ite cleric Nimr Baqr al-Nimr

The grotesque, medieval, oppressive, repressive, dictatorial, draconian Saudi Arabia where, recently, Saudi Arabian civilians were executed and crucified[28] for having committed the crime of thinking differently and protesting peacefully.
According to BBC[29]:

A Saudi prisoner has been executed and crucified, according to a statement by the country's state media.
The man was one of 37 people executed on Tuesday on charges of terrorism.
The statement added that the men were charged with 'adopting terrorist extremist ideology, forming terrorist cells' and harming the 'peace and security of society'."

Even if the charges were corrected (Saudi Arabia doesn't have a real or independent judicial system), that would be too extreme, no? To behead and to crucify individuals for the ideologies they might have inside their brains? Really? Only ideas, not actual crimes? And they were beheaded? Really?

In China, people with "terrorist extremist ideology" go to reeducation centers where they learn languages and professional skills. And the West goes wild about it! And the same BBC calls it "concentration camps":

Source 30 - China's hidden camps - BBC News

All I ask of the postmodern BBC liars is to explain to me what kind of mental process occurs in their brains that makes them see a concentration camp where there's a modern reeducation school? How do you do it? English classes and Chinese classes with whiteboards and desks. Kitchens for cooking classes were the Uighurs under reeducation have access to butcher knives. High-quality athletic spaces. And so on. How do you manage to see "concentration camps"?

Can't the BBC journalists understand how offensive is their pathetic comparison to the real victims of real concentration camps during WWII? Do BBC journalists understand English? Do they even know the definition of "concentration camp"?

Here's the definition provided by Oxford Dictionaries[31]:

"A place in which large numbers of people, especially political prisoners or members of persecuted minorities, are deliberately imprisoned in a relatively small area with inadequate facilities, sometimes to provide forced labour or to await mass execution. The term is most strongly associated with the several hundred camps established by the Nazis in Germany and occupied Europe 1933–45, among the most infamous being Dachau, Belsen, and Auschwitz."

Leave China alone and search for terror somewhere else closely related to the UK and the US: Abu Ghraib[32], Bagram[33] or Guantanamo[34].

Learn about all the horrific crimes[35] committed by the Contras in Latin America, where they tortured, raped, mutilated and killed defenseless human beings at the request of the US Terror Empire.

Source 36 – CIA/CONTRAS - Psychological Operations in Guerrilla Warfare

Learn about the millions of Indians the savage British Empire starved to death on purpose.

The list of British and US terror against humanity is endless!

And read articles like *Were there Irish slaves in America whose positions were far worse than African slaves?*[37] to find out how Westerners used to treat human beings from Africa, Asia or America.

Anyway, the United Kingdom and the United States sponsor and spread Islamic terrorism (backed by ultra-conservative Muslim movements such as Wahhabism and Salafism) and, together, act as world's police exporting "democracy" and "freedom" by dropping bombs and shooting guns. But that's "okay". France lets Saudi Arabia and Qatar inject millions into schools of fundamentalism to turn Muslim French citizens into terrorists. But that's "okay". The Chinese, with their millennial wisdom, implement prevention rather than cure, only to be accused of creating alleged "concentration camps". Moreover, the comparison is not even the most accurate because the West does not cure anything, the West inoculates viruses and bacteria in its victims and then, while beating them, they declare to be healing them.

But let's go back to Saudi Arabia. In Saudi Arabia, in spite of the horrors mentioned above, *everything is alright* and this barbarian country doesn't need "regime change", nor murderous embargoes or criminal sanctions. As long as the kingdom of ultimate terror and barbarism purchases weapons, tanks, and fighters, they will be left alone.

Yesterday in Venezuela, Edgar Zambrano, vice president of the opposition-controlled National Assembly, lost his immunity after a court decision. Then he was charged with having participated in the failed coup and was finally arrested. In reaction and in total disrespect of International Law, Washington interferes in the affairs of a sovereign nation to threaten it with "consequences". According to The New York Times[38]:

> *"Maduro and his accomplices are those directly responsible for Zambrano's security. If he is not immediately freed, there will be consequences."*

Two weeks ago, as previously mentioned, 37 peaceful protesters were beheaded in Saudi Arabia with no consequences whatsoever. Is it normal? Does it make sense in the neural circuits of Western brains? Apparently yes, as Western sheep-like humans lost the ability to reason and because, of course, their privileged standards of living are sustained by selling enormous amounts of weaponry to the very same Saudi criminals. I'll give you some examples.

Two days ago, according to France 24[39]:

> *"France confirmed contested arms shipment to Saudi Arabia."*

Two weeks ago, Turkish TRT[40] reported that:

> *"The UK and Saudi Arabia agreed on the sale of 48 British-made Typhoon fighter jets, in March 2018 despite Riyadh's involvement in Yemen."*

In 2018, according to Reuters[41]:

> *"Spain signed a $2.2 billion framework deal to sell warships to Saudi Arabia."*

Back in 2017, according to CNBC[42], "US-Saudi Arabia sealed weapons deal worth nearly $110 billion immediately, $350 billion over 10 years".

*

Look at these savage Israeli soldiers shooting an unarmed Palestinian civilian, at distance, for no reason, and celebrating it:

Source 43 - Israeli sniper appears to shoot unarmed Palestinian man in Gaza

Look at these mentally sick Israeli soldiers shooting an unarmed and utterly scared Palestinian girl:

Source 44 - Palestinian young woman pleaded her innocence but Israeli army still killed her

Look how psychopath-like *Israeli soldiers shot a blindfolded, handcuffed 16-year-old Palestinian boy in a West Bank village*[45].

Look at Thailand, a US ally where a military dictatorship has been ruling the nation for the last 5 years; where, a few days before the faked general elections, in response to the promises of some candidates to reduce the military budget, the commander in chief of the armed forces ordered[46] to pass on the radios controlled by the army the sadly famous song "Scum" ("Nak Phandin" in Thai), a symbolic reminder of the massacre[47] that took place at the University of Thammasat in 1976 (where an unknown number of socialist and communist students, unarmed and protesting peacefully, were surrounded and then slaughtered[48] by the Thai naval forces, by the Thai police and by the monarchy-sponsored extreme right-wing militia[49]: the Village Scouts[50].

In the West, only those who do not want to know or who have lost the ability to reason don't understand the subliminal message behind the order to pass the gruesome song "Scum" on the radio.

Fortunately, in Thailand there are rebellious citizens with a much better memory than most of their Western counterparts, creating equally rebellious rap songs like "What my country has become" ("Prathet Kumee" in Thai), whose video clip is a reenactment of the famous images captured during the 1976's massacre:

Source 51 - RAP AGAINST DICTATORSHIP - Prathet Kumee

Look at the Indonesian genocide in Papua, which I have already mentioned in Chapter 4.

Look at the carnage and the starvation of millions of people in Yemen, which I also mentioned in Chapter 4.

And so on. The list purposely omitted and censored by the Western prostituted media is almost endless.

*

And if you want to go back in time, learn about the horrible oppression that people in Pinochet's Chile (US-sponsored barbarian dictatorship) endured. Learn about the decades of horrible genocidal and terrorist oppression in Nicaragua, Panama, El Salvador, etc., all the result of US invasions, US coups d'états and US-sponsored dictatorships. Read, for instance, *What Uncle Sam really wants*[52], by Noam Chomsky.

*

And because we are dealing here with repression, I want to expose three very serious examples committed, respectively, by fascist-progressive Canada, by supremacist Australia and by the terrorist empire of the United Kingdom.

The first two come in reaction to the pathetic lies (very well debunked by Investig'action[53]) about Indigenous people being repressed by Maduro's government. Unlike Brazil, where even nowadays Indigenous people are raped, tortured, mutilated, sold, enslaved and murdered with total impunity (Bolsonaro promises to do worse, much worse! Overtly!), in the Bolivarian Republic of Venezuela, thanks to the outstanding Constitution of 1999, Indigenous people have the right to make their voices heard for real! Yes, they do, and for that purpose they can, for instance, select eight of their members to represent them in constituent assemblies, chosen not by a Western-like democratic vote, but in the way they find the best, in accordance with the principles of regulation of their societies, which are very different from the ones used in the *Westernised* urban Venezuela! Bravo, bravo, bravo, a million times bravo to the socialist, truly humanist and democratic Bolivarian Republic of Venezuela!

Let's talk about the indigenous people of Canada and Australia, these progressive "paradises" where extreme racial supremacism reigns, steeped in shocking chauvinism and fascism, especially in Australia.

CANADA - In Canada, Native Americans are constantly humiliated and oppressed, suffering real horrors infinitely more serious than the imaginary horrors supposedly "committed" by the Venezuelan "regime".

Kidnappings, rapes, assassinations, and even beheadings[54]. All things are possible. All this can be done against Indigenous people of Canada without any reaction from the "progressive" Westerners, confirming that I am right when I nickname them "Western human-like sheep". Otherwise, if they are so shocked with fake news about faked oppression in Venezuela, why are they not shocked by the fact that 25% of women murdered[54] in Canada in 2015 were indigenous, in a country where the indigenous population is only 1.1% of the total population[55]?

AUSTRALIA - A country where racial cleansing and cultural genocide are still common practices, as can be seen in the appalling documentary *Utopia*[56] (2013) produced by the great journalist John Pilger. In the sixties, to take aboriginal children away from their parents and consequently deny a future to their ancient societies, the white Australians used an incredibly supremacist excuse: the need to educate those children and to convert them to Christianity. In 2013, the trending supremacist excuse was the need to protect Aboriginal children from their "pedophile" parents. Too absurd to be true? No. This is real. This is happening in Australia, right now. Watch *Utopia!*

But kidnapping aboriginal children to deliberately execute a cultural genocide is not the only crime the ultra-racist and supremacist white Australian society committed against the Native Australians. There's so much more terror to expose! The systematic rape of Aboriginal women by white men, with total and shocking impunity. Nuclear tests (conducted by North Americans) on humans beings (Native Australians) without them knowing. Everything is possible in that savage nation named Australia. Choose what kind of barbarism shocks you the most and try to find it in Australia! I bet you will.

To learn more about these horrendous crimes committed by white Australians against the Native Australians, watch this list of documentaries produced by the fearless and deeply humanist Australian journalist John Pilger: *Pilger in Australia*[57] (1976), *The Secret*

Country: The First Australians Fight Back [58] (1983), *Welcome to Australia* [59] (1999) and *Utopia* [56] (2013).

UNITED KINGDOM - By far, the all-time world champion in the categories of imperialism, looting, destruction, genocide, and many other horrors. Yes, I know Western readers in general and British readers in particular, will find this sentence too harsh. I'm sorry, but it is true. Thousands of articles wouldn't be enough to produce a decent summary of all crimes the UK and its people committed against other human beings. As Vltchek wrote, *Lock up England in Jail or an Insane Asylum!* [60].

But well, there's no room for all their crimes in this article. Let's talk about a single crime.

I chose a blatant crime against humanity never mentioned in Western media and, therefore, completely unknown by the Western audiences: the tragedy of the Archipelago of Chagos, a nation occupied by imperial UK whose entire population was forced to leave their homes and lands and was then dropped in the slums of Port Louis, the capital city of Mauritius, where they have been surviving (not living) for dozens of years. Meanwhile, the UK illegally rented their homeland to the US, where this terrorist nation built, has and uses military bases! Do you know a worse example of oppression and repression? No? So leave Venezuela alone!

Source 61 - Stealing a Nation, by John Pilger

Less than three months ago, a *UN court rejected UK's claim of sovereignty over Chagos Islands* [62]. Western sheep-like humans didn't notice it because they were euphorically injecting anti-Madurism into their veins. The UN insists that the islands are not part of the United Kingdom and, if they are not part of the United Kingdom, the United Kingdom cannot rent them to third parties. The criminal UK must remove the North-American bases and return the islands to their legitimate owners.

But no, they never gave it back, and they never will. The United Kingdom does not give a shit about the UN, or about International Law, or about human rights, or the right of self-determination of a nation the UK has trampled underfoot. And so do its people. And so do westerners.

Western sheep-like humans don't know and don't care, and they hate those who know about the crimes of the British Empire and who expose those crimes. All you can hear, coming out of their instrumentalized mouths, is: "Putin is bad, Kim is crazy, Maduro is a dictator and... baa."

*

Finally, let's talk about clear and real repression in Venezuela. Repression by the opposition against those who dare to think differently and inform their audience.
What about Abby Martin and Mike Prysner receiving "hundreds of death threats and threats they would be lynched"[63]? And threats of being burned alive[64] by the terrorist "opposition"? Nothing about these violent threats on Western MSM? Of course not! And of course, Western sheep-like humans don't give a shit about journalists who risk their own lives to report the inconvenient truths about Venezuela.

Source 65 – RT report on the threats against Abby Martin and Mike Prysner

Western sheep-like humans only want to hear about *the brute devil with big mustache mistreating his hopeless plebe, and about socialist monsters eating little children for breakfast in Venezuela.*

The main subject of this book is Venezuela but, if in this chapter about repression and oppression, I hardly spoke of this country, it was because I do not waste my time analyzing emptiness! It wasn't a mistake. I just can't talk much about what doesn't exist. The idea was to show the readers some horrible examples of oppression and repression in the US, in the West and in other parts of the world where the US injected fascist and genocidal regimes, to finally ask the same readers: have you ever seen something similar perpetrated by Venezuelan police forces or Venezuelan armed forces? No? Then stop listening to imperial propaganda. It's a waste of time to listen about lies when there are so many truths yet to be explored!

PROTESTS
12.05.2019

In France, there are only civilians protesting against the government, hundreds of them wounded as a result of aggressions committed by the repressive French police forces. Worse, sometimes, when "protesters" burn or destroy something, it turns out that those who did so are infiltrated policemen, illegally destroying property and shamefully blaming peaceful civilians for what they have done themselves, in complicity and with the perverse support of Western Mainstream Media.

Source 1 – French policemen infiltrated in the protests

But there is nothing new under the sun since. As early as 2011, also in total disregard of its fundamental laws, the US government spied[2] and infiltrated secret agents in the civilian protests of "the 99%" and "Occupy Wall Street", for the very same purpose of sabotaging and eliminating peaceful and fair dissent[3].

Also very old is the North American propaganda of "regime change", as old as the depressing gullibility of Western sheep-like humans who swallowed and keep swallowing all the US crimes committed in the name of private "national interest".

Changes implemented to destroy democracies, socialist democracies or, at least, democracies independent from Yankee's imperialism. Changes brought to replace functional democracies by horrendous and genocidal military dictatorships in which *Contras* were trained in the School of the Americas to spread terror and sufferance among the poorest of the poor, all this with total impunity.

I don't see many pro-government demonstrations in France, so I can assume there are not many people supporting Macron. Nevertheless, Macron was democratically elected and we must respect the (pathetic) decision made by the French people when they elected an obvious agent of neoliberalism to (des)govern France. However, do not forget that France is not as democratic as Venezuela, since they do not have laws to revoke elected presidents using referendums as Venezuela does (read again the end of Chapter 1).

On the other hand, I do see many millions of Venezuelan civilians participating in pro-Maduro demonstrations...

*

In 2014, during Yankee's coup in Ukraine, Ukrainian police officers were burned alive with military flammable liquids, but, back then, the Western sheep-like humans were too busy talking about state repression to realize the "victims" where criminal oppressors and the "oppressors" were being burned alive without even fighting back.

Source 4 – Extreme violence of "peaceful" protesters against Ukrainian policemen, 2014

In 2011 in Syria, policemen were shot dead in the streets of Homs and Daraa with weapons supplied by Saudi Arabia through Jordan, and the Western Lying Media were shamefully talking about state repression.

In Venezuela, policemen are killed in bombings attacks, and pro-Maduro civilians are burned alive in the streets of this brave nation, only for Western Lying Media to totally ignore it and keep talking about state repression.

However, in Israel, snipers shoot dead[5] peaceful Palestinian protesters (even hopeless farmers working near the protests) in cold blood, at distance, while the Western Lying Media keep saying Palestinians are terrorists and, consequently, the claustrophobic apartheid and the slow-motion holocaust Palestinians are victims of... *is surely their fault* (fault of the Palestinians victims) and not of the fascist genocidal Israelis.

In both cases, Venezuela and Israel, Western MSM openly pick the aggressor's side and ignore or minimize their crimes.

Look at the total impunity with which Israeli fascist occupants killed[6] an unarmed human being in cold blood who, at the time, was doing absolutely nothing[7], just standing somewhere.

However, in France, genuine protests, peaceful protesters, defenseless protesters, are all being brutally[8] beaten up and losing eyes victims of rubber bullets shot by the oppressive regime forces with the intention to harm. When faced with this gruesome reality, Western sheep-like humans opt to call the oppressed victims *"lazy thugs"*, or simply ignore the repression going on in France.

No, don't tell me you're confused, dear westerners! You are not, you just have your brain functions completely shut down. You stopped thinking. You no longer think logically. You can't process information, you can't have sequential thoughts. That's the problem!
I have already said it, but I repeat it. Until today I have not seen a single picture of police repression in Venezuela. Only the opposite. Since the beginning (in 2013) of the supposed "oppression" and the real criminal economic aggression sponsored by North Americans and Europeans that our prostituted media shamefully dub as economic "crisis", Venezuelan policemen have been beaten, attacked and even murdered by terrorists "protesters".

What there is not in Venezuela, there's in excess in France. While the West and their vassal states (such as Brazil under Bolsonaro, or Argentine under Macri) keep slandering and attacking Venezuela, and accusing the great Venezuelan democracy of being a "dictatorship" where "oppression" reigns, none of them dare to criticize the French regime that has been ostensibly oppressing and mistreating its own people for the last 6 months.

But who cares, right? Western sheep-like humans either swallow the propaganda and call the Yellow Vests "troublemakers" and Maduro "oppressor" or, even worse, they claim to be confused! Bullshit. Not confused! Simply brain-dead!

For those brain-dead westerners and "confused" westerners, I have here something very simple to propose. I don't need to write extensive argumentations. Instead, I will share here a lot of data to be analyzed. Brain-dead westerners and "confused" westerners only have to compare the pro-Maduro and the anti-Maduro protests, without forgetting ethnic, racial and socio-economic variables.

Yeah, let them compare, because unlike France, in Venezuela there are the two types of demonstrations. And more, even though prostituted Western MSM only show the anti-Maduro side, the pro-Maduro protests are far greater in number than the anti-Maduro ones! Yes, it is shameful, infinitely shameful. The Orwellian reconstruction of reality carried out by prostituted Western MSM is unquestionably shameful!

Obviously, I am being ironic. Western sheep-like humans would never *waste* a second of their life learning how wrong are they about Venezuela.

But you, reader of this book, if you are reading this provocative and confrontational work, you surely are looking for something contradicting what MSM tells you all the time.

If you are really looking for objective information, start by comparing the peacefulness of the songs and the posters used by pro-government protesters, with the Molotov cocktails the anti-government protesters throw and with the assassinations anti-government protesters also commit:

Source 10 - Massive Pro and Anti Government Protests in Venezuela

Pro-Maduro Protests

Peaceful people like this, pro-Maduro, pro-democratically elected government, and pro-Bolivarian Socialism are never shown on propagandist Western MSM. As if media's obligation to "inform" was not to show both sides, but rather pick one of them! Not only they did so, but they also picked the wrong side, the one provenly sponsored[11] by the imperial US to bring chaos, misery, and death.

I will stop with the words and move on to the images and videos of these millions of pro-Maduro protesting in the streets of Venezuela. Many millions, often more numerous than the anti-Maduro, and absolutely peaceful, unlike the murderers, criminals, and terrorists that can easily be found in anti-Maduro protests:

Pictures:

Sources 12, 13, 14, 15, 16, 17 - Six pictures showing peaceful pro-Maduro demonstrations
Sources 18, 19, 20, 21 – Set of pictures showing pro-Maduro demonstrations, shared on social media

Videos:

Sources 22, 23, 24, 25, 26, 27 – Set of videos showing pro-Maduro demonstrations, shared on social media

Articles:

I could share a lot more articles and a lot more images but it's not worth it because, whoever is reading this book now, surely has an Internet connection at home or on his/her mobile phone:

In Images: Venezuelan People Mobilize In Support of Maduro [28]
Chavistas celebran aniversario del Caracazo *con marcha multitudinaria* [29]
#TrumpHandsOffVenezuela Concert Underway with over 150 Artists [30]
Dissecting the jingoistic media coverage of the Venezuela crisis [31]

Anti-Maduro Protests

Killing and attacking people always with covered faces. Burning, destroying and causing as much chaos as possible. Burning everything and everyone: tons of food, buses, hospitals, universities, subway stations, police cars, policemen and even civilians! For the terrorist "opposition", it is even "allowed to burn human beings alive! They commit all these unspeakable crimes and, imagine, they got and keep getting money from Europe and the US to continue committing these crimes. And Western sheep-like humans will never watch it or learn about it on Western MSM.

Pictures:

Sources 32, 33, 34, 35, 36, 37, 38, 39, 40, 41, 42, 43, 44, 45, 46, 47 - Sixteen pictures showing anti -Maduro demonstrations
Source 48 – AF's photo gallery
Sources 49, 50 – Two tweets showing violent anti-Maduro demonstrations

Videos:

Watch the documentary *Abby Martin Meets the Venezuelan Opposition*[51] produced by Abby Martin (if possible, watch the entire playlist[52] of documentaries this American journalist created to show us what's really going on in Venezuela):

Sources 53, 54, 55, 56, 57, 58, 59, 60, 61, 62, 63, 64, 65 – Set of videos showing opposition's extreme violence

As you can see from these videos, the Venezuelan right-wing terrorists and their pathetic puppets clearly get mad and lose their minds with the fact that the profit made with Venezuelan oil (righteously nationalized) is being spent to build public schools and universities, subways stations, public roads, and public buses.

One does not see clear examples of terrorism in the footage I shared above only if one conscientiously decides not to see it.

Books

Read! Read books about Venezuela and pay attention to the data provided:

Abril golpe adentro [66]
Abril sin censura [67]
Abril, Memorias de un golpe de estado [68]
Del terrorismo petrolero al golpe económico [69]
Facismo, el rostro oculto de la oposicion venezuelana [70]
La guerra contra el pueblo [71]
Venezuela se respecta - Derechos humanos en revolución [72]
Venezuela se respeta - Universidades víctimas de la barbarie [73]
Venezuela se respeta [74]
Victimas de la Arrechera [75]
Victimas de la Guarimba [76]

I would highlight a book with the list of victims of opposition's acts of terror that took place between 2016 and 2017, and remind the reader that, at the time, prostituted Western MSM never hesitated to blame Maduro's government for those very same deaths:

Víctimas fatales de la violencia política – Abril-Julio 2017 [77]

The big problem is that they cannot explain how the hell almost all the victims were pro-government, military personnel or policemen and that the few anti-government victims died as a result of their own acts of terror. The only ones killed by Venezuelan police forces (on duty, protecting the Venezuelan state against terrorist or criminal acts), resulted in the arrest and trial of the policemen involved, proof that Venezuela is very democratic and, if it fails, the fail is in the arresting of policemen who received orders to combat terrorist attacks!

In France, the very opposite happens. In France, the police forces attack and harm peaceful protesters, and then lock their victims in prisons!

*

Do you still have doubts about who oppresses who? No problem, just continue to read this book. If, after having read this book and analyzed all the given sources, you still find yourself "confused" about Venezuela, well, in that case, you too might be a lost cause. In that case, you could join the club of those who "have lost the ability to reason".

Because there's no way to accuse Maduro or pro-Maduro protesters of crimes they didn't commit. And because there is no way to deny, conceal or justify the immensity of crimes committed by the terrorist opposition. But first, read the book. You still have a lot of facts and evidence to learn about and analyze.

*

One last point. Can someone possibly explain the Venezuelan opposition's alliance with terrorist states like the US and Israel, or with fascist states like Brazil or Colombia? Can someone explain their economic ties, mutual support or mutual worship[78]? Can someone explain any of this?

Sources 79, 80, 81, 82, 83 - Venezuelan opposition showing its ties with Israel and the US
Source 84 – Anti-Guaidó goes with pro-Israel

INTERFERENCE AND INTERVENTION

15.05.2019

The US Intervening and Interfering Everywhere

First of all, let me remind the reader the arrogant[1] US is the all-time world champion on the categories of Intervention and Interference. The US has done it and still does it all the time, all over the world, audaciously killing presidents, shamelessly bombing presidential palaces, illegally investing millions (through NED, USAID, etc.) in brainwashing campaigns to push citizens of other countries towards "regime changes", sponsoring genocidal massacres of millions like in Indonesia in 1965, cowardly invading dozens of countries with false excuses to totally dismantle their societies and transform them into primary-resources producers using slave work, etc., etc. Unfortunately, to humankind, the list of criminal and often terrorist US interventions and interferences around the world is absurdly long.

Furthermore, most US past interventions and interferences around the world, are not even secret and are very well-documented and proven facts thanks to the constant release of declassified documents by the US State Department.

For instance, in June 2017 the US state department finally released "declassified U.S. government documents on the 1953 coup in Iran. The volume includes fascinating details on Iranian, American and British planning and implementation of the covert operation"[2] that successfully removed the democratically elected socialist government of Mossaddegh (a US-UK crime known as Operation Ajax[3]).

As Malcolm Byrne[2] pointed out:

> *The publication is the culmination of decades of internal debates and public controversy after a previous official collection omitted all references to the role of American and British intelligence in the ouster of Iran's then-prime minister, Mohammad Mossaddegh. The volume is part of the Department's venerable Foreign Relations of the United States (FRUS) series.*

For decades, neither the U.S. nor the British governments would acknowledge their part in Mossaddegh's overthrow, even though a detailed account appeared as early as 1954 in The Saturday Evening Post, and since then CIA and MI6 veterans of the coup have published memoirs detailing their activities."

As you can see, this criminal US-UK intervention in Iran was even not a secret before the documents became publicly available. This is just an example. I could but I will not introduce thousands of other examples. Visit nsarchive.gwu.edu[4] and nsarchive2.gwu.edu[5] to start digging the truth, if you wish to do so. There's no excuse for Western ignorance about all these crimes. Most westerners opt to not know so Western Terrorism can carry on enslaving billions to collect the money required to artificially sustain and maintain Western's privileged standards of living. Let them be arrogantly ignorant!

Another example of US criminal interference happened 16 years ago in a country neighboring Iran: Iraq. In a memo that was written by Bush's Defense Secretary Donald Rumsfeld 1 year prior to the US invasion of Iraq, there's a recipe on how to start a war in that country[6] using fraudulent excuses:

"How start?
Saddam moves against Kurds in north?
US discovers Saddam connection to Sept. 11 attack or to anthrax attacks?
Dispute over WMD inspection?
Start now thinking about inspection demands.
Surprise, speed, shock and risk."

Other more recent examples of US criminal interventions occurred not far from Venezuela and, just like the previous examples, the plans were to destroy leftist democratic governments in Latin America and assure no leftist forces would be left alive to retake the righteous control of those nations.

In 2009, when Manuel Zelaya proposed a democratic process to review the Constitution of Honduras and add what is already common practice in Germany (no limit of mandates for the countries' "ruler"), the US penetrated Honduras with its troops and removed Zelaya.

During the same year, a very similar US intervention took place in Haiti:

Source 7 - [Act Out! 198] - Pirates of the Caribbean - Stealing Haiti's Future by Repeating Colonialist History

Then westerners wonder (or not) why Haitians beg for the *bad, imperial and expansionist* Putin to counter-intervene in Haiti (read *'Long live Putin!' Haiti opposition protesters burn US flag, demand Russian intervention* [8]).

Even more recent is the aggression against Nicaragua[9], where the US tries to sabotage a truly democratic and socialist government, using the very same old tactic of injected protests and propaganda. The US accuses the government of committing oppressive acts it doesn't commit against those paid by the US to indeed oppress Nicaraguan people. And to make the scheme look plausible, of course, the US counts on Western MSM to lie, deceive, manipulate, omit and recreate a parallel reality, just as they do with Venezuela and Syria.

In spite of being incredibly overused, the criminal US tactics and MSM lies continue to be very effective. Worse, not only they keep interfering and intervening, but they show themselves proud of the illegalities they commit and even talk loudly about it:

Source 10 – Inside America's Meddling Machine: NED, the US-Funded Org Interfering in Elections Across the Globe

Even worse. Their agents of criminal interventions and interferences can be caught[11] with weapons in Haitian territory and admit they were in a "US government mission", only for the very same agents to be escorted to the nearest airport while complaining of the VIP-like treatment they got. In a normal world, they would be arrested and interrogated. In the US, they would be mentally and physically tortured with no access to lawyers or medical care. In Haiti's part of US "backyard", US agents are caught and kindly sent back to the US!

Interventions and Interferences in Venezuela

Overconfident after having received information (probably erroneous, as I try to prove in chapter 14) about the existence of an important number of high-ranked military personnel ready to betray Maduro's government, on January 2019 the US administration finally ordered the implementation of the "regime change" planned one year before.

On January 23 (anniversary of a 1958 uprising that overthrew a military dictatorship in Venezuela), apparently coming out of nowhere, Juan Guaidó declared himself President of Venezuela without having been elected. Actually, not even a candidate in the presidential elections that had taken place 8 months before.

Unknown by 80% of Venezuelans[12], being the President of the National Assembly of Venezuela as member of the opposition with the majority in that assembly (what an amazing thing to be found in a supposed dictatorship), and following the orders of his Yankee bosses who for many years groomed him in US soil (we will learn more about it in chapter 13 fully dedicated to Guaidó's past), Guaidó auto-proclaimed his person the President of Venezuela and was immediately recognized as so by the US administration and by several of its client states.

As Sergey Lavrov, Russian Minister of Foreign Affairs, righteously noticed[13]:

The fact that US immediately recognised the self-proclaimed "interim president" of Venezuela is a tell-tale sign that they are directly involved in creation of a dual power situation. This is another gross interference in the internal affairs of a sovereign state."

From the very beginning of this latest US interference in Venezuelan affairs, it was precisely too obvious the US was "interfering". To create a parallel power, out of nowhere, in a country with already too many problems, was surely not an attempt to do any good there.

The US has no good intentions toward socialist Venezuela. On the contrary, the US has plenty of reasons to destroy this great example of living socialism and plenty of resources to potentially plunder in its territory.

Furthermore, the levels of greediness and madness among the US administration and the North American corporations are so high that they can't even hide their vampire-like faces, ready to suck the blood of Venezuelans and the Venezuelan oil. Actually, they proudly admit they interfere in all ways possible: diplomatic interference, economic sanctions, embargoes, electric sabotage, funding both peaceful and terrorist opposition. And they intervene with all they can and want, delivering, for instance, "nails & wire for barricades" disguised as humanitarian aid[14].

Or infiltrating their agents among the fabricated and violent protests the Western MSM Orwellianly label as "peaceful":

Source 15 - US marine embedded with violent guarimberos at the border of Venezuela

*

Then we have the sadly comic opportunity of witnessing US MSM actually making very bad jokes about US interference and US intervention in Venezuela. There's no limit for US arrogance. They sabotage the economy and peace of a rebellious country, they proudly admit they are doing so, they make jokes about it live on their own MSM, and we are supposed to swallow it? Not me, I will never swallow their crimes, I will never swallow their criminal lies and I will never swallow their outrageous arrogance and lack of empathy towards the victims of their own crimes. But I would barf if I were to watch their televised terror-praising jokes for too long.

Other Orwellian bullshit we were supposed to swallow was the nonexistent Russian intervention in US elections. Thankfully, as Lee Camp stated:

"The Mueller report is done and it is not recommending any more indictments and it shows no collusion with Russia and it has made our mainstream and half our politicians look like idiot conspiracy theorists worse than when they all did the WMD chacha."

Thankfully, the truth came out and we can all expose servants of the Terror Empire (aka the US) like the vile Rachel Maddow. She really deserves to be exposed[16].

But let's not be naive. These incoherent beings, even after having been exposed for having lied about "Russian interferences" that never took place, and even after having been seen celebrating real US interferences in Venezuela, they will continue with their perverted and hellish rhetoric. After the ultimate self-humiliating scenes we watched, Rachel Maddow goes on with their sickening attacks on Russia.

And other North American prostituted "journalists" and prostituted politicians will continue to interfere in Venezuela affairs, including calling live on TV for the assassination of Maduro! No, don't blame Trump, you simple-minded Western sheep-like humans.

Fox News broadcasted it, but the guest was a former Bill Clinton adviser who literally said: "He [Maduro] needs to understand that a bullet to the forehead may be his way out of Venezuela"!

If you don't believe, please watch it[17].

*

Let's be honest. Nobody with a functioning brain can deny we are dealing here with blatant US intervention and US interference in Venezuela. And let's not forget there's plenty of conscious US citizens aware of the crimes their country is committing against Venezuela. Read, for instance, these two brilliant articles written by Kevin Zeese and Margaret Flowers, two of the bravest US citizens defending Venezuela and who are currently trapped[18] inside the Venezuelan Embassy in Washington with no access to water, food and electricity[19,20].

*

Certain of the US interference/intervention, let's look at how the US does it.

To begin with, Yankees do it so carelessly and with such contempt towards non-US citizens, that they can't even spell[21] the name of their puppet correctly. Look how Trump wrote "Guaidó" just a few days after his self-proclamation as President of Venezuela:

Yankees show no respect whatsoever for Venezuelan sovereignty and for International Law. As a consequence of the US illegitimate decision to recognize its puppet Guaidó as President of Venezuela, the legitimate government of Venezuela decided to cut off diplomatic relations with the US and, consequently, gave 72 hours for the US diplomatic mission in Venezuela to leave the country.

The US refused to take its diplomatic personnel out of Venezuela, acting as a pariah state that doesn't care at all about International Law. Worse, according to US secretary Mike Pompeo, Maduro was already a "former president" with no "legal authority to break diplomatic relations" with the US! How convenient!

How easy: you pick a new puppet-president for a given country, then you don't play according to International Law because you no longer recognize the legitimate President and, finally, you order your puppet-president to "beg you" to start a military invasion (as Guaidó is doing now[22]) to bring the whole nation back to Stone Age!

Brilliantly pathetic... And illegal!

Source 23 - Mike Pompeo announcing US decision to conduct diplomatic relations with Guaidó

Even worse, the US threatened Venezuelan with bellicose language to convince Maduro's government not to do what they have the right to do: forcefully (yet peacefully) remove from its own territory the US citizens overstaying after the end of the 72 hours ultimatum. US bellicose language implied US citizens are special human beings with special rights and, if anyone in Venezuela would dare to grab an arm of a special being to pull him out of the US former embassy in Caracas, again, US would surely disrespect International Law and would retaliate with a full-scale war.

To prevent the escalation, bullied Venezuela waited patiently. Doing so, Venezuela showed us another kind of US intervention: North Americans can illegally stay in a sovereign nation as long as they wish, with their backs protected by US military interventionism. And the government of the nation in question has no word to say on that matter, or else...

Or else the US will do what its administration already decided to do with or without that pathetic excuse: to attack and invade Venezuela with its Terrorist US Army. No one hides this intention anymore. They even meet[24] with their chosen Venezuelan puppets to discuss how to do it, and then proudly announce it[25]!

Against International Law, US high-ranked military personnel go even further and call[26] for the Venezuelan Army to betray its own government and its own nation, and to join forces with the US aggressor.

Thankfully, after 20 years of Bolivarianism, Venezuelan citizens and Venezuelan military personnel are very well informed about US criminal past, they have a very good memory of the crimes the US inflicted upon their nation during the last 2 decades and are absolutely committed to defending their nation's sovereignty and a country where people (and not corporative greed) come first:

As always, the few low-ranked who fell in the US Machiavellian tactics of deception, poor them, they ended out betrayed and abandoned in some forgotten street of Colombia with no food and no shelter[28].

*

And what to say about the illegal interferences of the grumpy old woman named Europe in the internal affairs of sovereign Venezuela? Well, once imperialistic and bully-boy, always imperialistic and bully-boy.

A few days after the nonsensical Guaidó's self-proclamation as President of Venezuela, al-Jazeera[29] informed us that:

> *"Spain, France, Germany and Britain have given embattled Venezuelan leader Nicolas Maduro an ultimatum, saying the nations would recognise opposition leader Juan Guaidó as president unless he calls elections within eight days.*
> *'If within eight days there are no fair, free and transparent elections called in Venezuela, Spain will recognise Juan Guaidó as Venezuelan president', Prime Minister Pedro Sanchez said in a televised announcement on Saturday."*

The EU sent observers to the Presidential elections that took place on May 2018, who found nothing wrong. The EU, as the Orwellian dictatorship it is, might not appreciate acknowledging how democratic Venezuela is, but their dissatisfaction can't be translated into ultimatums and threats against Venezuela. International Law is there to prevent this kind of bullying. Sadly, Imperial Europe, like the Imperial US, does not give a shit about International Law and the international institutions (like the UN) it helped create.

When I say "Europe" I mean almost all Europe, not just its heralds of neoliberalism, but also their twin brothers from the faked leftist parties with whom they constantly share political power to obediently fulfill the orders received from the International Economic Dictatorship based in the West.

There are exceptions, sure, but the Western Lying Media, also obediently, omit and censor any kind of dissent in the West. Read what European LEFT[30] published 3 days after Guaidó's self-proclamation:

> "The Executive Board of the Party of the European Left (EL) expresses its absolute rejection of the coup d'état attempt in Venezuela. An attempt sponsored, subsidized and instigated by the Trump administration, (mired in internal problems) that seeks to impose a "president in charge" who suit them. This action, in addition to being contrary to the Constitution of Venezuela, is nothing more than an interventionist ruse to justify a military intervention commanded by the United States, after the unilateral coercive measures (sanctions)."

*

But let's go back to European interference and European attempts to intervene. According to RT[31], on February 11, "a six-member European delegation that sought to meet with self-proclaimed Venezuelan 'interim president' Juan Guaidó is being expelled from Venezuela after being accused by Caracas of coming with "conspiratorial purposes".

Can you imagine the other way around, a Venezuelan delegation arriving in Brussels to meet with a self-proclaimed European 'interim president' trying to put an end on the real dictatorship ruling the EU? Can you guess the consequences of such kind of acts in Europe? No? Well, André Vltchek can, and that's precisely what he did in one of his assertive tweets[32]:

"Venezuela kicked out/deported group of EU MPs who came to meet with treasonous US puppet Guaidó. Pity they did not get arrested. In many 'democracies' they would be treated as terrorists; trying to overthrow government. Enough of lecturing, Europe!"

What were they expecting? The same EU that constantly lies about Russian imaginary interferences in European affairs wanted to have its agents walking free in the streets of Caracas openly interfering in Venezuelan affairs? Give me a break! And Western sheep-like humans do not find all this illogical and strange? Poor hopeless Western zombies!

And what about the prostituted European politicians, do they understand the full implications of their acts? Apparently they don't, as we can confirm on a tweet posted by González Pons[33], a European lawmaker:

"Be aware! Our passports have been taken and we're being expelled from Venezuela. Bad manners and the only explanation is Maduro doesn't want us here."

They entered a sovereign nation to openly commit illegalities (even if they don't see it as so); they landed in an airport controlled by the legitimate Venezuelan authorities but, once out of it, they started recognizing another non-elected parallel power? Luckily for them, they were not arrested, only sent back to their dictatorial EU. What an amazing dictator Maduro is... Not!

Three weeks later, the government of Venezuela announced the German ambassador as 'persona non grata' for having interfered in its internal affairs when, together with other European diplomats, he went to Caracas Airport to meet with Guaidó, who had just returned from his Latin American tour (Strange dictatorship in which coup plotters can go back home without being arrested, and can even meet foreign agents helping them prepare new coup attempts!)

In an official statement, the Venezuelan Foreign Ministry explained:

"Venezuela considers unacceptable that a foreign diplomat ... plays a public role on its territory, which is more typical for a political leader, who clearly supports the conspiracy agenda of the extremist parts of the Venezuelan opposition."

Apparently, Europeans can't learn from their own mistakes or they are too arrogant to respect the sovereignty of non-Western nations! And they will never learn.

After this incident with the German ambassador, many others followed. Given the constant political and economic bullying coming from Europe, Venezuela has no other choice but to distance itself from imperial Europe. Venezuela must be pragmatic, as Maduro has been saying lately. The sooner Venezuela gets rid of Europe, the sooner it can start working on solutions to neutralize the negative consequences of this undesired but rather imposed divorce. While working on new economic partnerships to replace Europe, Venezuela will surely suffer, temporarily. Submission would make sufferance last forever!

*

Back to the US interference, the US chose a non-elected president for a sovereign state and they find it absolutely normal. Mueller Report proved all the allegations about Russian interference in US elections were false, but US politicians are still *crying* about it. To close the circuit, the US demands Russia and other sovereign states allied with Venezuela to not "interfere" in this nation (i.e., to stop having normal and legal relations with the legitimate government of Venezuela). Moreover, the US threats Russia and China for their continuous support of Venezuela, and its Secretary of Armageddon named John Bolton goes as far as complaining the Russian and Chinese actions implicate "serious consequences"[34] to Donald Trump's plans (not serious consequences for Venezuela, as the US doesn't give a shit about Venezuela), naively admitting the US is, as always, protecting their private "national interests" in the Latin American aggressed nation.

Some of the vampires behind those private "national interests" are too excited to keep their mouths shut, like Chevron and Halliburton, already cheering for US intervention in Venezuela: *Regime Change for Profit: Chevron, Halliburton Cheer On US Venezuela Coup* [35].

US companies can't wait to start plundering Venezuela. Neither does Marco Rubio: "Biggest buyers of Venezuelan oil are ValeroEnergy & Chevron. Refining heavy crude from Venezuela supports great jobs in Gulf Coast. For the sake of these U.S. workers I hope they will begin working with administration of President Guaidó & cut off illegitimate Maduro regime"[36].

Neither does John Bolton. Watch the interview[37] he gave to Fox Business.

As Professor Tim Anderson rightly points out, "Venezuela it's not just the oil" and there's much more[38] to plunder there.

And so the US will keep injecting weapons[39] into Venezuelan territory to free the *enslaved resources* the US corporations dream about. According to Democracy Now[40]:

"McClatchy is reporting Venezuelan authorities have uncovered 19 assault weapons, 118 ammunition cartridges and 90 military-grade radio antennas on board a U.S.-owned plane that had flown from Miami into Valencia, Venezuela's third-largest city. The Boeing 767 is owned by a company called 21 Air based in Greensboro, North Carolina. The plane has made nearly 40 round-trip flights between Miami and spots in Venezuela and Colombia since January 11, the day after Venezuelan President Nicolás Maduro was sworn in to a

second term. Bolivarian National Guard General Endes Palencia Ortiz said, "This materiel was destined for criminal groups and terrorist actions in the country, financed by the fascist extreme right and the government of the United States." This comes as the United States is openly pushing for the toppling of Maduro's government."

Give a look at the seized weaponry:

Source 41 – List and footage of seized weaponry

*

While the US administration keeps aggressing Venezuela in the diplomatic realm, backed by the Western MSM lies and manipulations in the realm of Orwellian propaganda, and while the several US war machines (Pentagon, CIA, etc.) try to smuggle weapons into Venezuelan territory, another big war is being waged against Venezuela: the economic war of sanctions, embargoes and frozen assets.

The US thug administration stopped buying Venezuelan oil and tries to force the rest of the world to do the same, threatening[42] both allies and enemies with severe consequences if they don't accept illegal orders (yes, illegal, only the UN has the power to do so, not the US, 1 of the 193 UN members).

According to Reuters[43], "The United States is considering imposing financial sanctions that could prohibit Visa Inc., MasterCard Inc. and other financial institutions from processing transactions in Venezuela", strangling the already weak Venezuelan economy victim of harsh sanctions and embargoes imposed by the US against International Law.

According to RT[44], The Bank of England blocked the Venezuelan government from withdrawing $1.2 billion worth of Venezuelan gold.

Also according to RT[45], "Citigroup [decides] to sell Venezuelan gold after Caracas misses buyback deadline due to US asset grab".

In the West, everything is allowed to economically try to kill Venezuela!

More, in my homeland, the Southern European Vassal State of USA (aka Portugal), the owners of a new bank named New Bank (Novo Banco in Portuguese) apparently are nor tired of playing dirty games. Novo Banco was created to replace BES, a bank that disappeared in the aftermath of the last global economic crisis, together with plenty of money. Government bailouts and all sorts of tricks were used (like all over the planet) to steal and enslave the plebe. Now, the target is Venezuela.

According to Telesur[46], Portuguese Novo Banco "kidnapped US$1.726 billion which were meant to purchase medicines, food and supplies". RTP, the Portuguese prostituted state media outlet, reports[47] it in a manipulative and dishonest way that leads the Portuguese plebe to believe Maduro is making it up and that p*oor Portugal* is being a victim of Venezuela's *madman.* The Portuguese government clownishly denies any involvement or responsibility, arguing it has no power to influence Portuguese banks[48] (although the Portuguese government bailed out banks during the global crisis). Actually, what the Portuguese government can't do is to explain why a Portuguese bank steals money from Venezuela. And neither can Portuguese prostituted state TV channel (RTP[49]).

The list goes on and on. Western Lying Media and Western sheep-like humans accuse Maduro of being incompetent and socialism of being ineffective. In truth, as Maduro keeps insisting, the problem is the economic war on Venezuela: the U.S. government blockade is an arbitrary action that has allowed bankers to grab more than US$30 billion[50] from the Venezuelan people so far.

Furthermore, the US plans to illegally give Guaidó's gang access to at least part of the US$30 billion stolen from the Venezuelan people, so these US-trained Venezuelan criminals could buy US weapons to help the US invade and plunder Venezuela. Brilliantly criminal!

The US administration believes to be above the Venezuelan constitution, above the Venezuelan people, above the UN Charter and above International law. But they are wrong. They can bully but they can't conquer Venezuela and Venezuelans by stealing all they have. And by the way, it will not be that easy to fully implement this mad plan[51]:

"The U.S. seized Venezuelan assets but will have trouble handing them to Guaidó. The main asset is CITGO, which owns refineries and gas stations in the United States. But CITGO is deep in debt. Its refineries depend on the heavy oil from Venezuela. It might well go into bankruptcy in which case the debt holders will take it over. At least 49.5 % will go to the Russian company Rosneft. The legal process will take years."

Yet, some stolen money might be already in the hands of Guaidó's gang. According to Jorge Rodríguez[52], the Venezuelan Minister of Popular Power for Communication and Information, $1 billion was transferred to bank accounts owned by the Venezuelan opposition.

*

There's yet another kind of interference, the sabotage of the Venezuelan power grid using electronic warfare and attacks on infrastructure[53], an issue to be analyzed on chapter 14.

Many other kinds of interferences and interventions are taking place in Venezuela, but well, there's no room here for all of them, and I guess you got my point!

Fallacious "Russian Intervention" in Venezuela

When in late March a "Russian Air Force Antonov-124 cargo plane and a smaller Ilyushin Il-62 landed at the main airport outside Caracas"[54] with "around 100 troops and tons of equipment", Western Lying Media went wild, and so did Western Imperial governments.

Faced with blatant US intervention in Venezuela, including economic blockade, weapons and agents smuggled into the country, and with US Army in Colombia and in the coast of Venezuela ready to attack and invade the brave Bolivarian nation, perverted Western world suddenly pretended not to know any of this and "saw" Russian interference in a routine visit of a Russian military mission to Venezuela.

The mission is a common event and absolutely legal after the deal signed between Russia and Venezuela in 2001, in conformity with Article 187.11 of the Constitution of the Bolivarian Republic of Venezuela[55]. As Maria Zakharova, spokeswoman for the Ministry of Foreign Affairs of the Russian Federation explained:

"The presence of Russian specialists on Venezuelan territory is regulated by an agreement between the Russian and Venezuelan governments on military and technical cooperation that was signed in May 2001."

Maria Zakharova added "they are involved in the implementation of agreements in the sphere of military and technical cooperation" and they will remain in the country "for as long as needed".

Western Manipulative Media read it as a threat against the safety of Yankee's backyard, but it is not, for many reasons.

First, "as long as needed" means "as long as needed" for the parties that signed the legal deal, and the US has nothing to do with it.

Second, the UN Charter does not mention anything about North American backyards. In Chapter 1, Article 2, UN Charter[56] explains: "1. The Organization is based on the principle of the sovereign equality of all its Members", clearly indicating to be no room in

International Law for any kind of US backyards, as Venezuela, Russia and the US must be seen and respected as equally sovereign nations.

Third, there's also no legal framework in the UN Charter for the exceptionalism and imperialism implied by the modern-time interpretation[57] of the Monroe Doctrine.

Fourth, "Western hemisphere" and "our hemisphere" are examples of Orwellian *newspeak*[58] expressions with no connection whatsoever with the real world.

The problem is the psychopaths running the US Administration have lost connection with the real world a long time ago. In a direct reference to Yankee's intervention in Venezuela, National Security Adviser John Bolton declared[59]: "Today, we proudly proclaim for all to hear: the Monroe Doctrine is alive and well". Sure, thank you mad Bolton for having officialized the fact you stand for the disrespect of International Law.

The statement was made as Bolton announced a new pack of sanctions against Venezuela that should become a warning to "all external actors, including Russia". Like Venezuela, Russia is a UN Member. Once again, dear mad John Bolton: it is against International Law to threat sovereign Russia for having economic ties with sovereign Venezuela.

Furthermore, John Bolton told[60] reporters outside the White House: "This is our hemisphere" and "It's not where the Russians ought to be interfering. This is a mistake on their part. It's not going to lead to an improvement of relations".

No, it is not! There are no hemispheres in International Law. The US does not own Venezuela and Russian have the right to be military present wherever Russians want to be, as long as they do it legally, which is the case.

Source 61 - Bolton reinvokes the Imperialist geopolitical ideology of the Monroe Doctrine

Furthermore, US Vice President Mike Pence told[62] reporters:

"The United States views Russia's arrival of military planes this weekend as an unwelcomed provocation."

Sure, the US views it as so, but it is not.

First, it is up to the Venezuelan government to define "unwelcomed" or "welcomed". Second, it might be a Russian "provocation" on Yankee's private "national interests" in Venezuela, but a legal one, signed and agreed with the Venezuelan government. Third, every nation on Earth should rise up and provoke Yankee's private "national interests", exposing those interests for what they are: an illegal policy of plundering sovereign nations in total impunity. Fourth, objectively, the US administration, happy or not, has no word to say about the legal presence of Russian military missions anywhere in the world.

*

The US is legally present in its vassal state (my homeland) named Portugal, with several military bases. Portugal is also home to NATO's Communications & Information System Services Agency[63], and everybody is happy about being part of this genocidal organization! Happily ignorant, of course. Although legally present in Portugal, the US poisons and kills[64] Portuguese citizens with radioactive waste[65] without their knowledge, proving once and for all that US allies are, by definition, disposable.

Watch the full report: Portugal: *US base in the Azores linked to inflated cancer rates, environmental damage*[66].

*

But let's go back to US military presence outside the US soil. The US has more than 800 military bases (no matter how Orwellianly they label some of them to cook the numbers) in at the least 144 nations on Earth. In many cases, they do it legally, as Russia does in Venezuela. To have hundreds of times more military bases in foreign countries than Russia shouldn't be a reason for Uncle Sam to criticize

Russia for having 100 military personnel in 1 country named Venezuela! No, it should be the opposite. It should be a reason to shut up and keep a profound low-profile.

Source 67 - The Empire Files: The Rise of History's Biggest Empire

In many other cases, the US does it illegally, invading and destroying countries without a UN mandate, to then stay there forever will utterly nonsensical and pathetic excuses such as "fighting insurgents" in Afghanistan" or "assure ISIS won't come back" to Syria.

If you are a Westerner, and you are reading this, and you don't get why the US (illegally invading and occupying countless nations) has no right to complain about Russian legal military presence in Venezuela, well, in that case, congratulations, you are also a member of the (not so) exclusive club of Western sheep-like humans!

Non-sheep-like humans are perfectly capable of detecting the incoherences deeply embedded in this US imperial rhetoric. For instance, in an exercise of logical reasoning, let's close our eyes to International Law and accept Yankee's assumption that Latin America in general, and Venezuela in particular, are *American's Backyard*.

If so, what are US troops doing in countries like Estonia, Latvia, Lithuania, Poland and Ukraine, all of them sharing borders with Russia? What hemisphere is that?

The US defying Chinese sovereignty by crossing the strait between Chinese Mainland and Chinese Taiwan happens in which hemisphere?

In which hemisphere is the US deploying an aircraft carrier and bombers[68] to send a "message" to Iran?

In which hemisphere does the US commit mass killing of Syrians, Yemenis, Iraqis, Somalians or Afghans?

And so on...

No way, the US rhetoric of "Monroe Doctrine is alive and well" and Venezuela is in "our hemisphere" is an utter example of Western irrational reasoning, mixed with Western exceptionalism and Western supremacist ideals.

From Russia came the expected and logical reply. As reported by Sputnik[69], Maria Zakharova said: "US President Donald Trump should first stand by his promise to withdraw American troops from Syria before calling on Russia to 'get out' of Venezuela".

The spokeswoman for the Ministry of Foreign Affairs of the Russian Federation stated that:

"Before giving advice to someone to leave from somewhere, the United States needs to implement its own concept of pulling out, in particular, from Syria [...] A month has passed [...] I would like them to clarify whether they have withdrawn or not? Before taking charge of the legitimate interests of other states, I would advise the US administration fulfil the promises made to the international community."

So, imperial and criminal US, please go search for illegitimate interventionism where you do commit it, and leave Russia alone!

*

In Orwellian West, everything is possible nowadays. On one hand, we have the US admittedly willing to intervene militarily in Venezuela, with Guaidó's masochist supporters misinterpreting article 187.11 of the Venezuelan Constitution to beg to be bombed and slaughtered. On the other hand, ignoring the very same article of the Venezuelan Constitution, the very same Guaidó's supporters demand Russian personnel to leave their country. And so does the US Administration. And so do prostitute Western MSM. And so believe Western sheep-like humans to be a fair demand. But it doesn't make sense... at all!

Source 70 - Opposition's banner

The article 187 of the Constitution of the Bolivarian Republic of Venezuela states that:

"It shall be the function of the National Assembly: (...)

11. To authorize the operation of Venezuelan military missions abroad or foreign military missions within the country."

This point 11 has nothing to do with what many prostituted Western "journalists" said and wrote. For instance, Hélder Silva[71] (he works for Portuguese RTP), while attending a ridiculously small protest organized by Guaidó in Caracas, said that[72]:

"Here [in Caracas] people asked to be activated the article 187 (...) It is the article that allows the National Assembly to give authorization to foreign military actions in Venezuela."

No, it doesn't. Bullshit! Obviously, it doesn't. Read it again! It can authorize the presence of foreign military "missions" in Venezuela. "Missions" and not "actions" as the Portuguese "journalist" lied! Military missions as the one Russia has in Venezuela, yes! Military "actions" against Venezuela, no!

No constitution in this world would allow such absurdity, and one must be insanely retarded to even consider such a possibility! Portuguese national TV, RTP, is an ocean of retarded beings!

And by the way, if RTP's journalists really want article 187 to be respected, in that case, please apologize to Russia for having labeled its very constitutional military mission in Venezuela as "intervention"! Shame on RTP!

And by the way, Hélder Silva also lied when he mentioned "thousands" of protesters. Panoramic pictures of the event prove[73] there were only a few hundreds of people rallying. Shame on Hélder Silva!

*

More. Those gullible Venezuelans begging to have their country raped by the US as Syria, Libya, Yemen, Iraq or Afghanistan, during the protest, and as we can read in one of their banners[70], also

117

proposed R2P Doctrine, Roldós Doctrine and TIAR Treaty as tools to thoroughly assure their nation gets raped!

Roldós Doctrine - The Roldós Doctrine was proposed by Jaime Roldós Aguilera[74] on September 11, 1980, during an Andean Community summit. Although Roldós Doctrine "holds that the international community's concern for a country's internal human rights situation is not a violation of the country's sovereignty"[75], it has no validity, it is not a doctrine recognized by the UN, it has absolutely no jurisdiction over Venezuela internal affairs.

TIAR Treaty - Inter-American Treaty of Reciprocal Assistance does exist, but Venezuela is not a member[76] of it, so I will even not bother to analyze it.

R2P - The Doctrine R2P (responsibility to protect) is a new concept the US State Department proposed through a UN committee and was the excuse the US and its client states used to create a "no-fly zone" in Lybia allowing them to rape this socialist nation the way they did. In his great essay *Syria: the human rights industry in 'humanitarian war'*[77], Professor Tim Anderson carefully analyzed all the dirty consequences of this perverted policy. I highly recommend you to read it.

*

Let's now talk about double standards in Western Lying Media when reporting interferences and interventions.

According to Orinoco Tribune[78]:

"The warship of the United States, CG James WMSL754, of the Coast Guard of that country, was located this Thursday May 9 at 18 nautical miles from the Port of La Guaira, in jurisdictional waters of the Bolivarian Republic of Venezuela, in violation of international maritime law."

President of Venezuela Nicolás Maduro said so and shared on social-media enough information to make clear the US did invade

Venezuelan waters. Several other members of the Venezuelan administration did the same[79]. And so did Venezuela state media.

According to Sputnik[80], a Venezuelan patrol ship approached the US vessel and convinced it to change course:

"After our radio communications, the USCG James became convinced in the necessity to change its course and left our waters", the Navy said in a statement."

Nevertheless, many Western media opted to manipulate the Western audiences with their typical half-truths and linguistic tricks, in order to pass the idea that "mad Maduro" went "mad" again. So easy! And it always works!

For instance, RTP, the Portuguese state TV, (dis)informed the Portuguese audience affirming[81]:

"Without providing evidence and without any confirmation coming from the White House, The Venezuelan Minister of Defense denounces what he calls a 'US provocation'. The EU Coast Guard ship is believed to have been only 20 km off the coast of Venezuela, and only a single mile from the country's territorial waters."

For RTP, the proved violation of Venezuelan waters by CG James WMSL754 is logically a "myth", but one with very precise figures.

For Orinoco Tribune[78], "For its part, the Bolivarian National Armed Forces (Fanb) dispatched the ship Yekuana, in order to dissuade the US ship from remaining in Venezuelan territory." The facts are available online, but Western MSM prefer to ignore them.

Source 82 - US CG James inside Venezuelan territorial waters
Source 83 – Radio communication between Venezuelan navy and US CG James

On the other hand, the same Western MSM that denied, ignored or downplayed the data confirming the US intrusion in Venezuelans territorial waters, are the same that didn't hesitate to blame Iran for a non-event! Fake news! At best, a badly prepared and badly sold US false flag operation to frame Iran.

The same RTP, word by word, wrote in the title of one of its articles: "Iran accused"[84]! Sure, so easy to accuse. Iran must be blamed for 7 oil tankers supposedly attacked in a UAE's harbor. Supposedly, some of the tankers were Saudi, or not. Someone made up this dumb story (I bet someone in the US) but forgot to informed UAE's government about the plan.

Maritime Bulletin reported[85] that "UAE officials condemned these rumors as 'fake news', insisting that nothing happened, and that the port is working without any accidents of any kind, let alone series of explosions and fires." Hilarious.

Saudis blamed[86] Iran for having sabotaged the mysterious oil tankers. Pathetic.

Source 87 - Houthis Strike Key Saudi Oil Pipeline Amid Growing Concern Over Nearing US-Iranian Armed Conflict

According to several Western[86] and Gulf media, the oil tankers might have been attacked in the waters of the Persian Gulf and not in a harbor. Or in the Strait of Ormuz! Maybe 2 Saudi tankers were attacked or not; maybe 4 tankers from the UAE were attacked or not; together or separately, who knows? No one can even confirm if the attacks really took place! Then there were images of a Norwegian ship name André Victoria[85] that received a powerful blow.

In total, zero oil spills, zero persons injured, zero deaths, zero lost ships, zero fires, zero harbors damaged, and zero everything!

In the end, this crappy attempt to frame Iran with a supposed example of Iranians sabotaging oil trade was a total disaster. A "very cheap provocation / false flag"[88], as Professor Tim Anderson wrote. An epic failure, brilliantly analyzed and explained by Tyler Durden in his article: *US Accuses Iran Of Attack On Saudi Tankers*[89].

It is ridiculously obvious the US is trying to frame Iran with a false flag of the same kind they framed Vietnam (Gulf of Tonkin) and many others. Iran righteously threatens to close Ormuz Strait (to make an oil embargo to the whole world), if the US-imposed global oil embargo on Iran goes on. Never Iran mentioned the intention to commit acts of sabotage. And there are no records of Iran doing so.

The US is flooding the region with a military build-up, while it "orders 'non-emergency' government employees to leave Iraq"[90]. Dutch and German military personnel are leaving Iraq[91]. Spain pulled its frigate from a US-led group in the region[92], blaming the US for having changed plans and arguing that Spain has no issues with Iran.

The pattern is clear. The US is ready to attack Iran and, if it does so, it will use a false flag operation to trigger the war!

And by the way, in the opposite sense, one week earlier, in the very same area, "an Iranian oil tanker carrying over 1 million barrels of fuel oil suffered a malfunction in the Red Sea off the coast of Saudi Arabia", Jon Gambrell reported[93] to AP. The overwhelming majority of Western MSM didn't make any mention of this proven fact. How comes? Double standards? Yes, definitely!

*

Finally, let me remind you that the US (and not Iran) is a truly terrorist nation. No, it is not my opinion, it is the logical conclusion any rational being will come out with when faced with all the very well documented US terror acts. I propose you to learn more about a single one, a clear example of US terrorism committed precisely against Iranians.

Source 94 - The moment that Iran Air Flight 655 was shot down by a US navy guided missile

On July 3, 1988, Iran Air's 655 commercial flight traveling between Tehran and Dubai was premeditatedly shot down by the US Terrorist Armed Forces, which did so by firing an anti-aircraft missile from the warship USS Vincennes.

The outcome: 290 dead civilians, 274 passengers (of whom 66 were children) and 16 crew members.

According to the US version, its armed forces allegedly mistook the Iran Air 655 with an F-14A Tomcat fighter from the Iranian Air Force! Sure! How *sophisticated* North Americans are (not)!

And then what? Even if it was an F-14A Tomcat of the Iranian Air Force? What right did the US have to shut it down? What were US warships doing there, thousands of miles away from their country? Seriously, what were they doing there?

I explain. They were part of an illegal naval blockade on Iranian oil tankers! Moreover, they were supporting the illegal Iraqi aggression against Iran that devastated this country and caused hundreds of thousands of deaths and injured!

And who was the President of Iraq back then? Uncle Sam's favorite bad boy at that time, Mr. Saddam Hussein, put into power precisely by the US! A puppet of US imperialism who accepted to directly destroy Iran through a full-scale war at the request of the US!

And what was the purpose of this US terrorist attack on an Iranian plane carrying civilian passengers? Very simple, to make Iranians understand the US was willing to do anything necessary to bend this rebellious state where, in 1979, a revolution took place against the US-sponsored dictatorship established in 1953. To push Iranians towards capitulation and make them accept a *rotten* peace with Iraq (the aggressor), in disadvantageous and unfair circumstances for Iran (the aggressed).

In the aftermath of this US terrorist attack that killed 290 Iranians in a commercial plane, what conclusions were taken? Well, the Yankees, despite acknowledging they committed the attack, they never admitted any responsibility for the attack! Does it even make sense? No, it doesn't! Consequently, Yankees never apologized for the terrorist attack they carried out, even though the US administration ended up compensating the victims' relatives with $ 61.8 million. Does it even make sense? No, it doesn't! Forget about reasonable conclusions!

Finally, and as the issue is US Terror, this article would not be complete without quoting what Mr. George D. W. Bush, then President of the United States, said about this US terrorist attack: "I will never apologize for the United States of America. Ever! I don't care what the facts are."[95]

HUNGER AND SANCTIONS

21.05.2019

As Henry Kissinger, one of the greatest terrorist minds of the 20th century once said: "Control oil and you control nations; control food and you control the people."

Exactly, no matter how many human rights and international laws must be violated in order to achieve that control of nations and people, it is indeed possible to control both, if one really follows Kissinger's recipe for plunder and genocide.

If the US interferes in Venezuela to control the amount of food available (as the US has been doing for years), sure the US can make Venezuelans starve and, by doing so, somehow control at the least some of them.

Western manipulative MSM tirelessly criticize the Venezuelan government for all the hunger in the country, but they never search for the real causes of hunger and starvation, fearing tumble upon Kissinger's Machiavellian truth: *we the US* control food, so *we the US* control the Venezuelan people.

So let's talk about hunger and starvation of Venezuelans, starting with a sarcastic video Max Blumenthal filmed in a wealthy neighborhood of Caracas, in which he exposes the contradictions of pathetic Venezuelan opposition and liar Western MSM, both incoherent critics of Venezuelan socialism and constantly blaming Maduro's administration for the imaginary lack of capitalism:

Source 1 - Max Blumenthal searches for communist dictatorship at Venezuelan luxury mall

Another precious video to expose the incoherences spread by Western Lying Media about the lack of food in Venezuela is *Caracas streets and stores*[2], filmed two months ago by Eva Bartlett. As we can clearly see, shopping malls are full of all kinds of goods! As we can clearly see, Eva Bartlett was not in starving Yemen but rather in bullied Venezuela that, in spite of the genocidal embargoes and sanctions that would wipe out the entire population of many Western capitalist states, manages to survive with dignity, proving socialism to be by far more effective than capitalism in providing access to goods and services, even under total economic siege.

Even under total siege, as Eva Bartlett shows us with footage taken in the streets of Venezuela, the poor Venezuelans can still access and afford to buy food in a country suffering hyperinflation[3] imposed from abroad and also by the anti-Bolivarian local private companies[4]:

Source 5 – Eva Bartlett buying vegetables in Venezuela

To completely understand why Western MSM lie and exaggerate the reports on lack of food and goods in Venezuela, and to understand the real reasons behind the lack of certain specific goods such as toilet paper or cooking oil, one definitely should follow the extensive work Abby Martin has been producing for Empire Files[6], in particular, the episode *Inside Venezuela's Markets: Propaganda vs. Reality*[7].

*

In a more comic tone, I would invite the reader to think about the ultimate contradiction in Venezuela. From the unparalleled documentary War on Democracy produced by John Pilger in 2007, to the most recent (and abundant) videos showing poor Venezuelans happy with the political system and rich Venezuelans *crying out* about "hunger" and "starvation", every evidence leads us to conclude that, at the least, the over-privileged Venezuelan elite does not starve (although their decisions of self-inflicted industrial sabotage, and the shutdown of their own factories, does make some poor Venezuelans starve) and, ironically, while complaining about the supposed lack of food, we can see them surrounded by princely luxury, mansions, fancy clothes, super expensive cars and so on.

This can be seen not only in the streets of Venezuela but also abroad, namely in Miami, USA. Or in the streets of London, as you will see. I propose you to analyze a photographed evidence of wealthy well-fed Venezuelans wearing expensive clothes and carrying super-expensive bags (Jet Set Travel Medium Tote, by Michael Kors, $377[8]), in front of their Embassy in London, while shouting "We are dying of hunger!"[9].

*

But let's get more serious and rewind some of the main events of the economic warfare implemented by the West to artificially create hunger in Venezuela. Let's go back in time, to 2013, when the most visionary mind of modern times, Hugo Chávez, died or was killed, and when the West had recently started its longest and toughest aggression ever on Venezuela.

At that moment, with Chávez dead (but not gone), the main short-term objective was to distance Nicolás Maduro from Hugo Chávez, in order to buy the minds and souls of Chávez's supporters and make them believe Maduro had nothing to do with Chávez (wrong, painfully wrong). To do so, Western and Venezuelan anti-socialism propaganda forced itself to be more incoherent than ever, praising Hugo Chávez for having been a true socialist and democrat, while bashing Nicólas Maduro for being a *moron bus driver* and a *dictator*. The problem is Western and Venezuelan media used to say the very same nonsensical lies about Hugo Chávez.

With Chávez dead and Maduro democratically elected the new President of Venezuela, terrorist "opposition" started to implement fear, destruction and death in the street of its own nation. Local elites started to attack the economy by closing factories, sabotaging distribution, exchanging all its savings to dollars and sending it to Miami, etc. The US and Europe increased their support (including financial) to the opposition, while imposing economic and mediatic war on this brave nation. Colombia, paid to be an executioner of Western terror, had an important role in the smuggling of Venezuelan goods to sabotage its economy. And so on.

To learn in detail how the economic war was waged against Venezuela, and because there's no room to explain it here, I advise you to read the book *The Visible Hand of the Market: Economic Warfare in Venezuela*[10], written by Pasqualina Curcio Curcio. The author explains with precision many aspects of the economic war, such as induced inflation or planned shortages[11]. With this book the reader can, for instance, understand why in a country where the total amount of money allocated to import medicines increased many folds, the medicines are not available: one way to achieve so is to have murderous Venezuelans companies increasing many folds the price of imported medicines, so the country spends far more dollars in medicines, but gets far less of it in its harbors. Read the book!

*

Since the arrival of Hugo Chávez, the nominal GDP of Venezuela grew from $97,239 million in 1999 to $334,069 million in 2011 (UN figures[12]), proving real socialism to be highly effective in creating wealth. In 12 years, Chávez's Venezuela saw its economy growing 3,4 times!

In the same period, my neoliberal country (Portugal), a client state of the US, went from $127,633 million to $245,120 million, not even doubling. Portugal suffered no embargoes. Portugal didn't suffer a coup d'état imposed by the US.

Portugal didn't have its main source of income completely blocked as Venezuela had during the wrongly labeled general strike of 2002–03[13], a true sabotage of oil production that started with the oil company "striking" (And not the workers. Isn't it amazing?), resulting in production of crude oil decreasing by 68%[14], or even more, due also to storage restrictions, the stoppage of 29 compression units in Lake Maracaibo, the stoppage of the activities of the Terminal Lacustre de La Salina abandoned by its staff and the electronic warfare delivered at distance by a US company (SAIC) disrupting and trying to destroy the very complex infrastructures involved in oil production.

The North American SAIC inflicted electronic warfare to destroy oil infrastructure to try to prove tanned people from the South (especially if socialists) can't handle modern technology. They couldn't be further away from the truth. Even under Western electronic sabotage, Southern engineers, brave Venezuelans, managed to manually stop the electronic aggression.

All this happened thanks to the former US-puppet government of Venezuela, as Venezuela explained:

128

On January 17, 1997, a company known as Informatics, Business, and Technology (Intesa) was formed and tasked with optimizing the structures of information technologies used by Pdvsa. This company was born with Pdvsa investing, and owning, a 40% share, while another firm – Science Applications International Corporation (SAIC) – owned the rest (60%).

From that moment on, the US had a high-tech company (SAIC) "that provides government services and information technology support"[15] infiltrated in the main Venezuelan oil company, Pdvsa. Their acts of electronic sabotaged are well documented in many books published by Minci[16], including this one: *Del terrorismo petrolero al golpe económico*[17] (in Spanish).

Source 18 - A visual explanation of the cyberattack

Having the Venezuelan oil industry sabotaged is not a rare event, and the 2002-03 attacks were not the only ones. For instance, do you remember what happened with Amuay Refinery in 2012[19], when explosions killed 48 people and injured over 100 more[20]?

But let's go back to economic statistics. With the rise of economic warfare in 2012, and full economic war from 2013 until today, the tendency was reverted and Venezuelan GDP sharply sunk, proving that, yes, socialism + claustrophobic economic war doesn't work! Socialism left alone does work!

In 2012, the Venezuelan nominal GDP was $331,457 million, slightly lower than in 2011. The estimated nominal GDP for 2019 is $76,458 million. All the gains obtained by Bolivarian socialism were neutralized by the Western aggression.

In the meantime, the Portuguese nominal GDP went from $216,488 million in 2012 to a *whopping* $239,473 million in 2019, a mere 10% increase that proves neoliberalism, even if left alone, does not work! And it will get even worse, there in Portugal, once they have finished with the full privatization of what the Portuguese Constitution declares to be Portuguese basic rights (education, health, etc.). Look at the numbers in Table 1[21]:

Table 1:

YEAR	1999	2000	2001	2002	2003	2004	2005	2006	2007	2008	2009	2010	2011	2012	2013	2014	2015	2016	2017	2018	2019
Portuguese GDP in millions $	127633	118706	121650	134704	165286	189444	197642	208750	240502	263249	244364	238748	245120	216488	226144	229995	199,182	205269	219748	238510	239473
Venezuelan GDP in millions $	97239	117676	123156	95570	83670	112189	143290	177531	221817	289741	237294	294282	334069	331457	228017	215296	260089	236116	143841	98466	76458

Socialist Venezuela caught up Portugal in the first 2 years

Oil war imposed by US on Venezuela

Portuguese GDP was now twice bigger (2003)

In 2010 socialist Venezuela had again higher GDP than neoliberal Portugal

VEN 50% bigger

Venezuelan GDP dropped sharply, under full economic war.

Portugal had in 2019 the same GDP it had in 2010, proving it will not go far with neoliberalism and total submission to IMF, WB and ECB.

Pensamientos Nómadas 2019

Source https://unstats.un.org

As you can see, the Venezuelan economy dropped to around $75,000 million now in 2019, at the same time Venezuelan government complains about the more than $30,000 million lost this year due to sanctions[22], embargoes and Venezuelan assets being frozen by the US and its client states. As Maduro said:

"I will not get tired of denouncing the theft of more than $30 billion[23] belonging to Venezuela by the United States Government."

Then tell me hunger is not the fault of the economic war inflicted on Venezuela, as Kenneth Rapoza shamelessly wrote for Forbes[24]:

"The ruling Socialists United of Venezuela is, point blank, the only reason why Venezuela is a mess."

Kenneth says this preposterous nonsense in a world tired of past examples of entire socialist economies destroyed by US economic warfare to make them fail and turn their citizens against their innocent (and also victim) governments. Kenneth says this preposterous nonsense in a time of infinite access to information (thanks to the Internet), where everybody can easily access US declassified documents explaining point by point how they did in Allende's Chile[25] or in Cuba all the time. How they purposely destroyed socialist economies and starved people, purposely expecting to turn the people against their socialist governments!

Source 26 - The Battle of Chile – Part 1
Source 27 - The Battle of Chile – Part 2
Source 28 - The Battle of Chile – Part 3

More: look how socialist and democratic Iran governed by Mossaddegh was starved the same way, and for the same reasons:

Source 29 - Iranian Prime Minister Dr Mossaddegh was overthrown by USA UK in 1953

And the list is painfully endless.

Still, Western sheep-like humans buy this lunatic rhetoric, as they want to believe! They want to believe "socialism is bad" and "Maduro is a dictator". Let them believe!

Yes, Venezuela's economy is in very bad shape, but there are no miracles! Venezuelan economy could now be many times bigger than the Portuguese if it were not a victim of endless economic war and other kinds of war. Sure the Portuguese economy could be bigger too, if it had a truly socialist government but, in that case, they would be the next victim. And Portugal under total economic siege would last a week at most, I bet! Portuguese would all starve to death, literally, knowing how exposed is their economy to World Economic Dictatorship's greediness and how dependent they are from imported goods.

Back to Venezuela, in the era prior to the full-scale economic war, it was not only the nominal GDP that was thriving. Standards of living and basic human rights too. There's plenty of data available online proving so, For instance, read *The Chávez Administration at 10 Years, The Economy and Social Indicators*[30] (by the North American *Center for Economic and Policy Research*, based in Washington DC) and amaze yourself.

For instance:

1. Thanks to the implementation of universal access to education (Misión Robinson I) in 1999, about 1.5 million Venezuelans have learned to read and write.

2. In December 2005, UNESCO declared illiteracy in Venezuela had been eradicated.

3. The number of children accessing school increased from 6 million in 1998 to 13 million in 2011, and school attendance reached 93.2%.

4. The Misión Robinson II (Mission Robinson II in English) was launched to increase secondary education. Thus, the school enrolment rate in secondary education rose from 53.6% in 2000 to 73.3% in 2011.

5. Ribas and Sucre missions allowed tens of thousands of young adults to reach college. Thus, the number of students in colleges rose from 895,000 in 2000 to 2.3 million in 2011, with the creation of new universities.
6. The National Public Healthcare System was created to guarantee free access to medical care for all Venezuelans. Between 2005 and 2012, 7,873 medical centers were established in Venezuela.

7. The number of doctors rose from 20 per 100,000 inhabitants in 1999 to 80 in 2010, an increase of 400%.

8. Misión Bairro Adentro I provided 534 million medical consultations. About 17 million people could finally get medical care, while in 1998 less than 3 million people had regular access to healthcare. 1.7 million lives were saved between 2003 and 2011.

9. The infant mortality rate decreased from 19.1 per thousand in 1999 to 10 per thousand in 2012, a reduction of 49%.

10. Life expectancy rose from 72.2 years in 1999 to 74.3 years in 2011. Thanks to Operación Milagro, launched in 2004, 1.5 million Venezuelans victims of cataract and other eye diseases have regained sight.

11. From 1999 to 2011, the poverty rate went from 42.8% to 26.5%, and the extreme poverty rate went from 16.6% in 1999 to 7% in 2011.

12. In the United Nations Development Programme (UNDP) Human Development Index (HDI) classification, Venezuela rose from 83rd place in 2000 (0.656) to 73rd place in 2011 (0.735), reaching the level of *nations with high HDI*.

13. The Gini coefficient decreased from 0.46 in 1999 to 0.39 in 2011.

14. The rate of child malnutrition decreased by 40% from 1999 to 2011.

15. In 1999, 82% of the population had access to drinking water. In 2011, they were 95%.

16. In 1999, only 387,000 elderly people received a pension. In 2011, they were 2.1 million.

17. In 1999, Venezuela produced 51% of the food consumed. In 2012, Venezuela was producing 71%, while food consumption had increased by 81% since 1999. If food consumption in 2012 were similar to that of 1999, in 2012 Venezuela would be producing 140% of the food required.

18. From 1999 to 2012, the number of calories consumed by Venezuelans increased by 50%, thanks to Misión Mercal, which created a chain of 22,000 food markets where products were subsidized on a 30% average. Meat consumption increased by 75%.

19. The rate of malnutrition dropped from 21% in 1998 to less than 3% in 2012.

20. The unemployment rate dropped from 15.2% in 1998 to 6.4% in 2012, with the creation of more than 4 million new jobs.

As you just read, when left alone (or not so much), revolutionary socialism can bring a sharp increase in standards of living (1999-2012). And even under harsh economic warfare, it still does. Until 2019, thanks to Maduro's government, 2.6 million homes have been built[30a] in Venezuela for the poor classes, and the governments of Chávez and Maduro distributed millions of hectares of land to its native population willing to farm.

But these are embarrassing truths to be totally and systematically censored by Western Lying and Manipulative Media.

These and many others. Western MSM refuse to report the private sabotage of food distribution but, when the Venezuelan threats to take control over the distribution of food, the Western MSM go wild and start crying out about *hellish* "forced nationalization".

Who in the Western MSM prostituted industry of propaganda cares if people are starving due to private sabotage, right? Actually, "starving Venezuelans" is always good news for them, a new reason to falsely accuse the Venezuelan government of others' crimes, right?

Who in the Western MSM prostituted industry of propaganda dares to mention CLAP (Local Committees for Supply and Production[31])? Who in the Western MSM dares to reuse all the data shared by CLAP on Twitter[32], Facebook[33] or Youtube[34]? CLAP is a network of committees (within the communities) charged with supplying and distributing food and it was created in 2016 in response to the economic sabotage.

Who in the Western MSM mentions food destroyed or burned by the opposition? Who in the Western MSM mentions food and oil being stolen and smuggled into Colombia?

And, because we are talking about the Venezuelan economy and its interactions with the outside world, why does the West totally ignores ALBA, UNASUR, PetroCaribe, PETROSUR and many other Venezuelans initiatives promoting transnational cooperation among the Southern nations and fighting for their true independence from US doctrines of imperial "backyards"?

These initiatives envisioned the end of economic colonialism of the South by the North, making it as self-sufficient from bullying North as possible, encouraging Southern economies to develop value-added products and internal consumption for those products, to stop being an enslaved source of half-stolen raw material to be sent to richer North. These initiatives Hugo Chávez came with, were meant to prevent what happened over and over in South America, so the great Fernando E. Solanas would no longer have reasons to produced appalling documentaries such as *Social Genocide* [35] or *Argentina latente* [36].

2019 Sanctions

If, as already explained, economic war always managed to inflict minor or major damages to the Venezuelan economy, a total blockade in 2019 cannot be seen as a *bright US idea to solve all the economic problems of bullied Venezuela*. Yet, Western sheep-like humans, when invited to swallow this appalling contradiction... they actually do it, and even ask for more!

The total blockade has its consequences, of course it has! But, somehow, Western sheep-like humans manage to ignore it and see Maduro's fault in every single empty stomach and empty shelf (real or imaginary, it doesn't matter).

No matter how the Western world blatantly prevents Venezuelans from accessing food and other basic goods, the *mantra* says is "Maduro's fault" or "socialism fault". But facts are facts[37]:

The US adopted sanctions against Venezuelan state banks[38] (like Venezuelan Economic and Social Development Bank[39]), preventing the government from buying necessary goods. Even The New York Times does not hide it in the title of one of its articles: *New U.S. Sanctions on Venezuela Aim to Choke Off Government's Finances*[40]. Yet, when Western MSM (The New York Times included) blame Maduro for the economic problems his country suffers, Western sheep-like humans completely swallow it and say "baa".

Today, Venezuela's Ambassador to Russia gave a press conference in Moscow[41] in which he explained in detail all the economic attacks on Venezuela and the negative consequences of having their money, gold and other assets stolen[42] by Portuguese or British banks, but who cares, right?

In the West, no MSM reports about press conferences delivered by Venezuelan officials. In the West, no sheep-like human even considers the possibility of watching and listening to such *hellish* press conferences. Their arrogant ignorance tells them they already *know* everything, they already *know* "Maduro is bad", "humanitarian" bombs are the solution and "socialism only spreads poverty". Their arrogant ignorance tells them to go watch fictional and crappy Western violence on Game of Thrones and to pretend real Western violence against Venezuelans is not happening. How *convenient* and *relaxing*.

The US and Europe know how dependent is Venezuela from its oil revenue. And so did Chávez. As Venezuelanalysis reported[43]:

> *"Hugo Chávez knew that Venezuela was very vulnerable. Its oil revenues account for 98 percent of its export earnings."*

The US and Europe know about this Venezuelan dependence, similar to any other country exporting goods and absolutely natural. Dependence on the need for money to satisfy ulterior needs: food, water, shelter, energy, etc. Westerners who ignore this fundamental truth surely have lost all their reasoning capacities. Many westerners are no longer able to extract logical conclusions from words and facts like[43]:

> *"The country relied on oil revenues to import food and medicines. The theft of the $7 billion in PDVSA assets, the seizure of the $1.2 billion in Venezuelan gold in the Bank of England, the transfer of ownership of the PDVSA subsidiary CITGO in the United States to the opposition and the pressure on oil exports squeezed Venezuela very hard. U.S. National Security Adviser John Bolton estimated that the United States (and Canadian) sanctions had cost Venezuela about $11 billion."*

And so, Western sheep-like humans - the majority -, are sure and certain that "it's all Maduro's fault"...

*

Let's now talk about very real starvation on an unspeakable scale: Yemen.

I will not explain here any of the reasons and historical facts behind the aggression against Yemen. In his article *The US-Led Genocide and Destruction of Yemen* [44], David William Pear brilliantly explained everything a reasoning and truly humanist mind needs to know about the Western-Gulf aggression on Yemen. So please read it. I will move on to the most important consequence: the many millions starving to death there.

If the US administration had an unlikely and remote interest on humanitarian aid, instead of providing Saudi Arabia with weapons and military assistance used to destroy Yemen, the US and its client states should punish Saudi Arabia with harsh sanctions and embargoes (instead of Venezuela).

If the US administration had a minimum concern about human life, it would not allow (let alone help, has it does) Saudi Arabia to destroy Yemeni harbors and Yemeni airports in which could arrive the food and medicines necessary to stop the imminent genocide (by starvation) of millions of Yemenis.

If the US administration does not care about the many thousands of Yemenis killed with US weapons and the many thousands of Yemenis killed by the Saudi blockade on Yemen (implemented with the use of US weapons), there's no logical argument to make any reasonable being believe the US somehow cares about starving Venezuelans.

The problem is: there are many people who have lost the ability to reason!

In the West and in many other clients states of the West, billions manage to self-inflict total ignorance about Yemen, total ignorance about the 2002 failed coup in Venezuela (2019's failed coup is almost a blueprint of 2002's coup), so they can conveniently be the *deeply committed humanists* they mistakenly believe to be when they express their outrage on the human suffering Maduro does not inflict on the Venezuelan people. And so they can become nonconscious[45] supports of US *humanitarian* bombs that would come after US fake humanitarian aid. And so I call them Western sheep-like humans.

Sheep-like humans are precisely what biased Western MSM need, so they can exaggerate the amount of Venezuelans starving, hide the real imperial reasons behind Venezuelan starvation and, of course, ignore accessible official information about the millions that are indeed starving to death in Yemen.

According to a report[46] published by UN News on February 14, 2019:

> *"An estimated 24 million people – close to 80 per cent of the population – need assistance and protection in Yemen, the UN warned on Thursday. With famine threatening hundreds of thousands of lives, humanitarian aid is increasingly becoming the only lifeline for millions across the country.*
>
> *(...)*
>
> *Thursday's 2019 Humanitarian Needs Overview for Yemen report, shows that 14.3 million people are classified as being in acute need, with around 3.2 million requiring treatment for acute malnutrition; that includes two million children under-five, and more than one million pregnant and lactating women.*
>
> *Highlighting that more than 20 million people across the country are food insecure, half of them suffering extreme levels of hunger, the report focuses on some key humanitarian issues: basic survival needs, protection of civilians and livelihoods and essential basic services."*

What else must be said to wake up those Westerners who *cry* for starving Venezuelans? What else? Force them to read the full overview published by the UN: *2019 Humanitarian Needs Overview for Yemen report*[47]? I don't think so. They only need to reason, but they can't.

And to force them not only would be a violation of their fundamental rights, but also an ineffective way to show them the obvious and real reality they provenly don't want to know about. Most of the people in the West (the Western sheep-like humans) don't want to know, only want to believe "Maduro is bad" and "socialism doesn't work".

So be it.

But the reality is still out there: millions starving to death in Yemen as a consequence of Western-Saudi terror; thousands feeling hunger due to the Western economic war on Venezuela.

Their Machiavellian Western MSM, sometimes, even offer them emotional warfare, approaching facts, showing them that yes, it is true, Yemenis are literally starving to death. For instance, look how the British SkyNews shows starving Yemeni children without explained the British government and the British Terrorist Army are (also) to be blamed:

Source 48 - Special report: Yemen's children are starving

This footage comes from the same parallel reality of Western MSM blaming Yemenis for daring to attack Saudi military bases with drones[49]! Yes, a parallel reality. A perverted parallel reality in which Western media like shameless France24 *cries* for the damages Yemenis cause in infrastructure used to exterminate Yemenis[50]: "the Sanaa strikes targeted nine military sites in and around the city, residents said, with humanitarian agencies reporting a number of casualties", or "the coalition described the drone attack as a 'war crime'." Really? How dare they?

Still, how can westerners manage not to link the dots? How is it possible the vast majority of Westerns do not notice the blatant contradiction between having Yemenis starving and having media blaming Yemenis for daring to resist? Well, probably because they become... Western sheep-like humans! *Voilà*! All they need is to read, in the same France24's article, that the bogeymen (the Iranians) are to blame: "Iranian-aligned movement", "Iranian tools", etc. And nothing else matters...

*

Back to Venezuela, another trending expression on Western Lying Media is "humanitarian crisis". Sure. The fault of the same Western economic war already mentioned here.

But even if not. Even if it was, in fact, a humanitarian crisis created by Maduro's alleged mismanagement of Venezuelan internal affairs. So what?

Why so much Western concern about the hyper-exaggerated "humanitarian crisis" in Venezuela when the Western populace barely show any concern about the horrendous humanitarian crisis of slave markets in raped Libya? Or about the fast-motion and deliberate massacre of native Papuans at the hands of the genocidal Indonesia Army killing defenseless human beings in the name of Western's companies and their *divine right* to profit from everything and over everyone's sufferance? Or about Afghanistan destroyed and colonized by Western armies? Or Syria suffering a genocidal blockade on energy, food, and medicines imposed by the same criminal European states than injected terrorism in Syrian soil and that bomb Syria anytime they want?

What is going on with Western brains? Selective humanism? Supremacist blindness? Total assimilation of fallacious anti-socialism propaganda? Normalization of genocide if it is to sustain their privileged social welfare systems? I insist, the problem probably is: Westerners have lost the ability to reason! If not worst!

Thankfully, there are still Western brains reasoning, like Lee Camp's brain, who constantly and thoroughly breaks apart Western anti-Venezuela propaganda:

Source 51 – Redacted Tonight 230: Venezuela Fake Coup, Truth About Kamala Harris, & Yellow Vests

*

If Western sheep-like humans were truly interested in exposing "humanitarian crisis", instead of blaming the victim (Venezuela), they should be blaming the aggressors (USA, EU and other brothers in crime).

Once done with it, they should move further. For a matter of coherence, they should start thinking about the US citizens living in total misery, exactly like the Venezuelans shown above. And ask themselves questions such as:
- How dare Western MSM to ironically call Venezuela a "socialist utopia", when neoliberal capitalist US has the very same kind of poverty?

- How can we conclude "socialism" is incapable of producing wealth if socialist states are constantly embargoed, sanctioned and attacked?
- How comes that hundreds of millions of human beings living in total misery in turbo-capitalist South East Asia is not enough for Western MSM to conclude capitalism is a big failure?
- Why don't Western MSM ironize about an Indonesian "capitalist utopia"?
- Why can't we see more examples of miserable US citizens in Western MSM?
- Why don't Western journalists take those real examples to start question capitalism the same way they take cooked examples to smear Venezuelan socialism or Cuban communism?

Here are some examples of what should be found in fair and honest Western MSM:

Source 52 - Homelessness and 3rd world conditions in Los Angeles
Source 53 - Alabama's sewage crisis

There are, of course, many more!

*

All this I said about US and about gullible Westerners, does not mean I deny the genocide that is happening in Venezuela. On the contrary, it is a fact, a well-documented fact. According to the Center for Economic and Policy Research[54] that recently published the report *Economic Sanctions as Collective Punishment: The Case of Venezuela* [55]:

"[US] sanctions have inflicted, and increasingly inflict, very serious harm to human life and health, including an estimated more than 40,000 deaths from 2017 to 2018; and that these sanctions would fit the definition of collective punishment of the civilian population as described in both the Geneva and Hague international conventions, to which the US is a signatory. They are also illegal under international law and treaties that the US has signed, and would appear to violate US law as well.

The Center for Economic and Policy Research and its personnel are not the only ones exposing this crime. Recently, Alfred de Zayas, United Nations Independent Expert on the Promotion of a Democratic and Equitable International Order, arrived at a similar conclusion:

"The American sanctions and the European Union sanctions [on Venezuela] are premeditated murder."

Yes, besides being illegal, sanctions and embargoes do kill, as people do not live without goods, and cannot buy goods without money, and there's no money available if there are sanctions and embargoes, as the article *Sanctions on PDVSA: the US Oil Lobby* [57] clearly demonstrates. The losses are not only direct, as consequences of embargoes and sanctions. Indirect losses such as lower prices for the oil Venezuela somehow manages to sell somewhere else represent also a big economic problem. If you look deeper, you will even find indirect losses outside Venezuela.

As well resumed by Abby Martin[58], "the US economic blockade of Venezuela already cost them $113 billion between 2013–2017 according to CELA[59]. The embargo asphyxiated the economy, prevented recovery & laid propaganda framework for military intervention."

Do you remember the figure of 40,000 deaths between 2017 and 2018? Now do the maths and calculate how many dozens of thousands were killed by Western Economic War on Venezuela during the period 2013-2017. And do not forget this multi-dimensional war on Venezuela begun much earlier, in the first day of Hugo Chávez in office, 20 years ago. For instance, read this very well elaborated resume about the last 5 years of US sanctions on Venezuela: *Timeline of Half a Decade of US Economic War Against Venezuela* [60].

Western imperialism got used to conquer and plunder and can't do anything about it. It can't stop thinking about plundering the country with the world's biggest oil reserve, with the world's second gold reserve and the world's fifth iron reserve, etc[61]. And to do so, first Western imperialism needs to denigrate, sabotage, destroy and exterminate the *bad* example the Venezuelan Bolivarianism represents.

And so it starves many. It starves many to death. It kills many...

*

As you understood, I am not here denying people are starving nowadays in Venezuela.

I'm here asking reasonable human beings to be reasonable and, if possible, Western sheep-like humans to also stop being *sheep-like* on Venezuela and to be just *humans* again, so we can all reasonably conclude what must be logically concluded: the inhuman monsters responsible for death and starvation in Venezuela are the *sanctioners* and *embargoers* running the interference-addicted US administration!

And none of this is new. As very well resumed by Venezuelanalysis[43], bully US imposing embargoes and sanctions on Venezuela is nothing new in this tenacious country, and the methodology is a blueprint of the murderous tactics inflicted on Allende's Chile and on all the other countless victims of US terrorist interventionism:

> *"The United States government and the Venezuelan oligarchy first tried to overthrow the Bolivarian Revolution in 2002. Great hope in Chávez prevented a discredited oligarchy from victory. Oil revenues then allowed Chávez to build up pillars of support for the revolution. But the depletion of the oil prices from 2009 threatened the Bolivarian process. Chávez died in 2013. The combination of low oil prices and the death of Chávez changed the political calculations.*
>
> *Egged on by the United States, opposition leaders Leopoldo López and María Corina Machado called for demonstrations against the newly elected President Nicolás Maduro in 2014. It was clear that the protests were intended*

as a provocation, drawing a crackdown from the government forces, which allowed U.S. President Barack Obama to sign the Venezuela Defense of Human Rights and Civil Society Act of 2014. This act allowed Obama to sanction individuals in the Venezuelan government. It was extended in 2016 and will expire—unless extended again—at the end of 2019. The sanctions policy was to be the new lever to pressure a vulnerable Venezuela.

In March 2015, Obama declared Venezuela a "threat" to U.S. "national security," an extreme step, and sanctioned a handful of Venezuelan government officials. The administration of Donald Trump only sharpened and deepened the policy. Obama sanctioned seven individuals, while Trump has—thus far—sanctioned 75 individuals. Obama forged the spear; Trump has thrown it at the heart of Venezuela."

And then there's the other kind of sanctions and interferences, equally illegal according to International Law. The sanctions the US usually imposes or threatens to impose on those who don't abide by US international illegality[62]. For instance, read the explanation for what Reuters calls "secondary sanctions": *U.S. presses India to stop buying oil from Venezuela's Maduro*[63].

But who in the West cares about International Law, right? US administration never did and, nowadays, openly, John Bolton even makes fun of it, referring to Venezuela in this preposterous manner: "The Monroe Doctrine is alive and well. It's our hemisphere"[64]. He said it all.

Worse. Look at what Reuters reported[65] two months ago:

"The United States will withdraw or deny visas to any International Criminal Court personnel investigating possible war crimes by U.S. forces or allies in Afghanistan, Secretary of State Mike Pompeo said on Friday."

The US not only doesn't give a shit about International Law (as was always the case) but now openly spits on it! Pompeo clearly admitted US administration sees itself above the law, unpunishable for crimes against humanity committed in Afghanistan, and with *legitimacy* to punish International Criminal Court personnel for doing their job. And there are still people out there genuinely believing the US wants to bring humanitarian aid to Venezuela? Seriously?

Source 66 – Mike Pompeo admits that in the CIA "We lied, we cheated, we stole..."

Today, the US doesn't care, doesn't try to hide it doesn't care, and doesn't care about what others think about this same US constantly breaking International Law. In fact, after having normalized disrespect for International Law, psychopaths like Pompeo, Bolton or Pence seem to be quite proud of their international misconduct.

And so they do it and keep doing it, perfectly aware of the very high chances their international criminality might result in big troubles for others. And all this does result in (often) tragic consequences for others, all over the planet! And they calmly admit it. And they keep doing it, no matter what!

Psychopaths? Of course they are! For instance, according to African Globe[67]:

> *"The United States government has, for the first time, admitted that the illegal sanctions it imposed destroyed Zimbabwe's economy and were hurting ordinary people.*
> *Incoming US Ambassador to Zimbabwe David Bruce Wharton made the admission yesterday at a media roundtable discussion in Harare and pledged to work with authorities in Zimbabwe and the US to normalize relations."*

What did they learn with the economic warfare they inflicted on Zimbabweans? Nothing: psychopaths!

What did westerners learn from having been manipulated about Zimbabwe? Nothing: sheep-like humans!

*

As Maduro constantly says, Venezuelans suffer immensely from the economic war the West inflicts upon them, but this is a transitory process for those who decided to confront the bullies (instead of kneeling). It is transitional torture that must be endured while the solutions for total independence from the imperial West are being built and tested.

Now Venezuelans are faced with hard times they didn't provoke nor asked for. It was imposed from abroad.

The economic siege is there, Venezuelans decided not to surrender... so now the only possible path is to seek true independence.

Measures are being taken to completely de-dollarize the economy; there are plans to trade using rubles[68], renminbi and more currencies other than the US dollar; the central bank of Venezuela is developing an independent national payment system to avoid being strangled by a Visa/Mastercard blockade; a cryptocurrency named El Petro was created, backed by Venezuela's oil price; the government established partnerships with Chinese investment banks and other banks from China, Russia, and other nations; the government looks for alternative markets in countries like Turkey that no longer abide by US dictates; in theory, China, another prime victim of US sanctions, could buy the entire production of Venezuelan oil.

Once this process is completed, Venezuelan will be in a much better situation: economically independent from the US and Europe. Venezuela never asked for it; Venezuela was forced to have it. If it succeeds, no one in the West will compensate Venezuela for the inflicted losses and sufferance the Venezuelan economy and the Venezuelan people had to endure. But Venezuela will no longer be exposed to the risk of being bullied by Imperial West.

The economic independence will be politically and militarily backed by the emerging nonconformist forces: Russia, China, Iran, and others.

As a result, we will live in a two-blocks world, with the West and its plundered client states on one side, and the non-submissive nations all united on the other side. Now they are only a few, but soon many more will join them, as soon as they find a way to do so.

Many now understand that being allied with Russia and China is the only option available to not end out like Libya. And it is a good positive option. Many in Haiti beg Russia to intervene, to restore democratic order and expel the Western plundering forces that now occupy and enslave them (read: *'Long live Putin!' Haiti opposition protesters burn US flag, demand Russian intervention*[69]). Many more will follow.

Source 70 - Protests in Haiti

Until then, while still struggling for economic independence, Venezuela will surely suffer many US crimes against humanity, increasingly more obvious and more absurd, although it is hard to imagine a lower attack than the latest one under preparation: "U.S. Prepares Charges, Sanctions Over Venezuela's Food-Aid Program"[71]!

Yes, the US administration is preparing an attack[72] on CLAP, a program to provide food to those in need. US is preparing to sanction CLAP, a project that was precisely created to fight the hunger and sufferance the US interferences brought!

Source 73 - The Real 'Humanitarian Aid' in Venezuela: Govt Supplies Food at Affordable Prices to Local Residents

Yes, the US is ready to sanction humanitarian solutions[74] created to face previous US sanctions[75]!

Yes, the US is ready to target native humanitarian help with more sanctions[76], so Venezuelans can starve to death and Western sheep-like humans can shout: "I told you, Maduro is a genocidal dictator!".

No, the US is not sanctioning the Venezuelan private distribution companies behind the artificial shortages of food and medicines.

No, no Western MSM reports the fact that, often, the availability of certain goods drops while the levels of production or importation are, in most cases, constant.

Those companies are private and - here is the problem, Maduro's government has no control over their artificially-created shortages. Nationalize those companies and a big part of the problem could be solved. Or, at the least, impose regulations over the prices to end with artificially-inflated prices, as many in Venezuela ask for[77].

Venezuelan socialism brought CLAP to fight private artificially-created shortages. The US does not attack those responsible for the shortages. The US attacks the socialist government trying to solve the shortages with CLAP and other measures. The US adds international blockade to assure people in Venezuela will be left without essential goods.

This is not the right way to prove "socialism doesn't work". This is the right way to prove socialism works too good to be tolerated by neoliberal imperialism and, therefore, must be slaughtered and starved to death!

HUMANITARIAN AID

26.05.2019

Every serious publication on "humanitarian crisis in Venezuela" should definitely include a resume of what was exposed by Max Blumenthal, Anya Prampil and Alfred Zayaz at a side event at a UN Human Rights Council session in Geneva on March 19.

To leave no doubt about their intentions, the title of their presentation was "Humanitarian crisis in Venezuela: Propaganda vs. Reality"[1].

During the 40 minute presentation, the panel provided very clear evidence that: 1st, the "humanitarian crisis" in Venezuela is exaggerated by Western MSM; 2nd, the "humanitarian crisis" happens in result of the actions of those supposedly willing to deliver "humanitarian aid"; 3rd, it is not true Maduro's government is to be blamed for the "humanitarian crisis"; 4th Maduro's government actually does what it can to counter the "humanitarian crisis" inflicted on the Venezuelan people by foreign powers.

*

As the Russian ambassador to the UN affirmed[2], during the Security Council meeting that took place following the beginning of the (failed) coup in January 2019:

"It is no secret that the current economic crisis is provoked by the countries that are the first to cry on behalf of the Venezuelan people."

Western governments may lie and propagate lies their Western sheep-like humans easily swallow. That's fine. But one must not forget the world is composed of far more nations than those in North America and the EU. In the remaining countries (the majority, by the way), there are plenty of people not swallowing this latest Western "humanitarian aid" paranoia.

Source 3 - China maintains that all countries should abide by basic principles of international law

They don't swallow it because they saw and have plenty of evidence about the true nature of Western "humanitarian aid" for "regime change" or for "Arab Springs". For instance, they know and they can prove Western "humanitarian aid" for Aleppo (late 2016) was to be delivered to organizations classified as "terrorists" even by the same Western governments trying to give them "humanitarian aid". And they can prove the Western "humanitarian aid" intended to be delivered to terrorist organizations spreading death and destruction in Syria included weapons that are not humanitarian aid[4]. Weapons in the hands of internationally recognized terrorists can only help spreading more death and destruction, which is in total contradiction with the concept of humanitarian relief.

Venezuelans are aware of these facts and do not want to be the next victims of Western "humanitarian aid" of smuggled weapons to trigger bloody civil wars. Actually, Venezuelans already caught[5] Western "humanitarian aid" trying to introduce materials to be used in violent uprisings or even in a civil war.

As we witnessed during the pathetic attempt of coup d'état on April 30, US[6] and European weapons smuggled into Venezuela were used by coup-plotters to shoot[7] life ammunition against the police and military forces defending the sovereignty of Venezuela.

So no, thank you but Western "humanitarian aid" no!

This kind of bellicose "humanitarian aid" would only lead to violence, death, and destruction!

*

So, dear not dear US administration and its obedient vassals, forget about your "humanitarian" aid being delivered to Venezuelans.

But, if by any chance I am wrong about your "humanitarian" intentions, in that case, please deliver it somewhere else.

For instance, you, the US administration, you could repack the refused "humanitarian aid" and give it to the victims of the wild capitalism you injected in Honduras after the 2009 coup d'état you also executed there! Since you interfere in the Honduras administration, it would be a piece of cake to make your "humanitarian aid" enter Honduran territory.

Moreover, it would make a lot more sense to have the US sending humanitarian aid to Honduras (instead of Venezuela), as it is well known that a good part of the migrants of the caravans trying to reach the US is precisely composed of Hondurans, precisely running away from the US-imposed capitalism that always brings poverty!

Or even better, send you humanitarian aid to Yemen where, according to The New York Times, *85,000 Children in Yemen May Have Died of Starvation*[8].

But you need to multiply your humanitarian aid hundreds of times, as the number of people in need there, thanks to US-UAE-UK-Saudi state terrorism, reaches 14 million.

Or bring it to Congo. Or to Nigeria, Borneo, Papua, Sudan or to so many other hopeless victims of Western economic terrorism and Western military terrorism.

I know, bring it to a country named Peru, so close to Venezuela, where extreme capitalism created an abundance of miserable and desperate human beings living in absolute poverty and surrounded by a collapsing and totally poisoned environment (all consequences of "utopian" capitalism[9]).

*

According to The World Counts[10]:

"Every second a person dies of hunger. Right now, more than 1 billion people suffer from hunger. This means that 1 in every 6 people on Earth don't get enough food to live a healthy life. This year 36 million of these people will die of hunger!"

Every second one person dies of hunger, many of them in North America and Europe, most of them in plundered and enslaved countries victims of North American and European turbo-capitalism. So why do Westerners suddenly care so much about "starving Venezuelans"?

You should know the answer by now.

*

Back to the Venezuelan crisis, it is true many people suffer now from the lack of certain products and medicines, but in Venezuela, there's no need for "poisoned aid" as Professor Tim Anderson rightly labels the US supposed "humanitarian aid":

On February 14, a few weeks after the beginning of this latest *coup season*, Telesur reported[11] the arrival of at least 64 containers[12] with twenty-five million euros-worth of humanitarian aid. 933 tons[13] of medical supplies sent by "Cuba, China, Russia, Palestine, Turkey, among others".
"Over 22,570 units of spare parts for medical equipment, 192,000 kit for diagnostic tests and 'more than 100,000 kits for cytology' were included in the shipment", added Telesur.

We have here clear evidence proving Western MSM lie when they accuse Maduro of refusing humanitarian help and, consequently, being "responsible" of many deaths. Wrong, absolutely wrong. Liars!

In a few years under Bolivarian socialism, the Venezuelan healthcare system went from a third world level to a decent and modern level, and the many millions that never had visited a doctor in their lives, now they can do it anytime they need, not far from their home's door.

It is true that many hospitals are now empty, but not due to mismanagement, lack of doctors and nurses or inadequate equipment. No. Hospitals are closed or empty because genocidal West inflicted a criminal blockade on Venezuela, preventing this country from acquiring medicines and all the other materials necessary to run a hospital.

Worse, as declared by Venezuelan Ambassador to Russia Carlos Rafael Faria Tortosa[14], 1,5 billion dollars belonging to the Venezuelan government and deposited in a Portuguese bank to purchase medicines and medical equipment in Europe, were stolen by Portuguese Novo Banco.

Confronted with all these horrible facts, how dare Western MSM in general, and Portuguese MSM in particular, to blame Maduro for the death of thousands of Venezuelans who didn't get proper medical treatment? Have they all lost the ability to reason?

If not, if westerners haven't lost the ability to reason, in that case, they should force their governments to stop with this genocidal embargo and send genuine humanitarian aid as Chinese did again a few days ago.

According to Sputnik[15]:

> *"A second Chinese cargo plane carrying 71 tons of aid including medicine arrived in Caracas on Monday as part of a "humanitarian technical" cooperation agreement between President Nicolás Maduro's government and Beijing."*

And in case you missed it, very recently, the Chinese government offered medical supplies, a medical team, US$800,000 in cash and 10.000 tons of rice[16] to help the victims of Cyclone Idai that ravished Zimbabwe. Oh, devil Chinese creatures, always trying to help hopeless human beings without asking anything in return! How dare they! No wonder we, the West, experts on humanitarian bombs, humanitarian wars and faked humanitarian aid, hate so much the Chinese and boldly call them the "yellow threat"! Yes, yes, shame on us the West!

*

In any case, sovereign and independent Venezuela has all the right to refuse humanitarian aid, genuine or not. Venezuelans remember how the US went to Haiti to "help" the victims of a hurricane and, suddenly, the US was militarily occupying Haiti.

But even if Venezuelans knew nothing about US military humanitarianism, why couldn't they refuse humanitarian aid? Why can't they refuse humanitarian aid? Why do Western MSM do so much noise about it? Why all this faked empathy for suffering Venezuelans when there's always so little empathy for the billions right now suffering in countless manners, all over the planet?

Why all this faked empathy for suffering Venezuelans, now, when we do remember how little some Western MSM cared about the 2010 Israeli vicious attack against a flotilla carrying humanitarian relief[17] that was supposed to reach Gaza?

Source 18 – IDF Boarding Gaza Aid Flotilla

Why all this faked empathy for suffering Venezuelans, now, when we do remember how scandalously some Western MSM manipulated the facts and recreated a narrative in which the unarmed volunteers ended up portrayed as the "aggressors", while the terrorist Israeli soldiers who killed unarmed civilians became the odd "victims" of their own illegal assault on a civilian flotilla, in international waters, and carrying humanitarian aid?

Source 19 - Israel Attacks & kills Activists on Freedom Flotilla with Aid for Gaza

*

I could not end the subject of the "Venezuelan humanitarian crisis" and "refused humanitarian aid" without mentioning the ultimate dark irony. Sure Venezuela refused faked bellicose "humanitarian aid" offered by the US, now in 2019. But the USA also refused Venezuelan and Cuban humanitarian aid in 2005, when many people lost their lives, victims of the exceptionally devastating Hurricane Katrina.

According to The Guardian[20], in 2005:

"An offer of aid from the Venezuelan president, Hugo Chávez, which included two mobile hospital units, 120 rescue and first aid experts and 50 tons of food, has been rejected (...)"

The same happened with the proposed Cuban aid, as Shane Quinn reminded[21] us many years later:

"Cuban leader Fidel Castro offered to[22] ship over 1,600 doctors and dozens of tons of medical supplies to the US's affected areas. Considering the decades-long terrorist attacks perpetrated against Cuba by US governments, in addition to a crippling embargo, it was a noble gesture by the Castro government."

In his essay for Mint Press News, Quinn gave us a hint for the reasons behind the US administration decision to refuse genuine aid in times of catastrophic human tragedy:

"Surely Cuba's vital aid to Pakistan (and others) in its hour of need did not go unnoticed by US President George W. Bush. However, it had already been deemed more important by his administration to preserve the superpower's prestige rather than protect its own citizens."

Of course, the US couldn't let a socialist nation and a communist nation help saving lives of US citizens, as it would be an extremely inconvenient proof that socialism and communism are not what US propaganda always told us to believe.

The US has spent hundreds of millions of dollars in Contras[23], in terrorist attacks[24], in the Operation Mongoose[25], in acts of sabotage, in invasions, in genocides, in coup d'états, etc., all over Latin America and in the rest of the world, to be able to (wrongly) prove socialism and communism "do not work". How in the world would the US administration open the *gates of truth* to save *mere* several thousands of *disposable* human beings, many of them black?

Fidel Castro resumed it very well:

"The American government's pride dictated that their own citizens had to die on the roofs of their houses, or on the roofs of hospitals from which no-one evacuated them, or in stadiums, or in nursing homes where some of them were given euthanasia in order to prevent a horrible death by drowning. That's the country that portrays itself as 'a defender of human rights'."

Fidel Castro was not exaggerating, as Naomi Klein proved years later in her outstanding analysis on the US imperial machine of capitalist terror: *The Shock Doctrine: The Rise of Disaster Capitalism* [26].

In this book, Naomi Klein exposed the true murderous and inhumane nature of the US Empire. Here is a glimpse of the many inconvenient truths about Hurricane Katrina she unraveled in *The Shock Doctrine*:

"The work was extraordinarily slow, and bodies were left in the broiling sun for days. Emergency workers and local volunteer morticians were forbidden to step in to help because handling the bodies impinged on Kenyon's commercial territory. The company charged the state, on average, $12,500 a victim, and it has since been accused of failing to properly label many bodies. For almost a year after the flood, decayed corpses were still being discovered in attics."

Many people suffered and died in avoidable circumstances. A truly socialist state cares about its people and when there are humanitarian tragedies, people must come first, no matter the economic price, as Hugo Chávez proved us during the Vargas tragedy[27] in 1999.

In an inhuman and vulture-like society as North Americans, unfortunately, live in, money comes first, no matter how many people unnecessarily die. So be it, but you the bloody US administration leave Venezuela alone and mind your own genocidal businesses...

VIOLENCE

30.05.2019 - 06.06.2019

False Humanitarian Aid has been used to promote violence in synchrony with violent and criminal "opposition" funded with dozens of millions of US dollars.

Violence is incredibly common in Venezuela but not as the West portrays it. The West never reports crimes like the one that happened a few days ago, when a Venezuelan policeman was shot dead[1] in the streets of Caracas.

What is the percentage of acts of violence with US dollars behind it? Surely high, Eva Golinger and other researchers already proved. But who cares about real facts and real reality in the West, right?

There is more than enough data to prove the US has been spending hundreds of millions of dollars in South America alone. A good part has been spent in illegal US interventions and interferences in Venezuela, invested in NGOs, civil society organizations, criminal organizations, movements like Súmate, new political parties and so on, to create anti-socialism dissent and foment "regime changes" recurring to extremely violence (call it "terrorism") and even coup attempts.

As exposed by Jean-Guy Allard and Eva Golinger in their book *USAID, NED y CIA - La agresión permanente*[2] (2009, in Spanish):

"Through an Office of Transition Initiatives (OTI), which was established in Venezuela in August 2002, USAID has invested 15 million dollars in the political conflict in Venezuela during the last year and a half. And it plans to invest 13 million dollars more in 2010 (...). These millions of dollars fuel the conflict in the country, maintaining different opposition groups alive and helping to create new organizations to continue their destabilizing plans. The beneficiaries are well known: Súmate, Sinergia, CEDICE, Red de los Barrios, Primero Justicia, Consorcio Justicia, Universidad Metropolitana, Liderazgo y Visión, CESAP, and hundreds of other political groups, NGOs and political parties that live off the money and support that come from Washington."

Primero Justicia is the political party whose presidential candidate in 2012 and 2013 elections was Henrique Capriles Radonski (he lost to Chávez, then to Maduro, respectively, in presidential elections considered fair and transparent by many international observers such as the North American The Carter Institute, as well as by the OAS).

Henrique Capriles Radonski is famous for his many crimes and for his constant calls for violent uprisings against constitutional and democratically elected governments. Already under a Bolivarian Venezuela with Chávez as president, Capriles won several elections but never had the idea to label his own victories illegitimate or fraudulent or whatever he calls PSUV's[3] victories. He was Mayor of Baruta from 2000 to 2008, and then governor of Miranda State from 2008 to 2017!

Unbelievable, I wonder what Western prostituted journalists would say if they had to explain how this man from the "oppressed" opposition managed to be elected so many times under the "dictatorship" of Chávez and Maduro. But they don't. Western prostituted journalists are not paid to do journalism nor to be coherent!

In Chile's Pinochet, for the *crime* of thinking differently, socialists were electrocuted, thrown to certain death from military helicopters, tortured and killed in all the ways possible. Many thousands disappeared or were killed. In Chávez/Maduro's "dictatorship", anti-socialists like Caprile are *magically* allowed to participate in, and even win, democratic elections? Am I missing something here or what?

In November 2008 Capriles became governor of Miranda after winning democratic elections. He took the seat that until then belonged to Diosdado Cabello, one of the right-hand men of Chávez who had to hide himself during the 2002 failed coup, as the hoards of savage "opposition" members like Capriles wanted to capture him dead or alive. The coup failed.

The President Hugo Chávez and the vice-president Diosdado Cabello recovered the power 2 days later. Why, in this "horrendous" Chavista dictatorship, nobody decided to rape Capriles' wife in front of him? Why did nobody decided to torture Capriles and then throw him out of a helicopter? How did Capriles manage to win democratic elections and be a governor of a state, taking the seat of Diosdado

Cabello that he, Capriles, and his fellow criminals, tried to purge? Am I missing something here or what?

Capriles, abusing of his powers as mayor and governor, manages to commit all kinds of crimes, like vandalizing an embassy, destroying cars belonging to Cuban diplomats, cutting off the water and electricity supply of the Cuban Embassy and blocking it, preventing Cuban ambassador German Sanchez Otero from leaving the embassy, etc.

Come on, Capriles himself, invaded the Cuban Embassy[4], violating International Law!

But what do they say in Western Lying Media and Venezuelan Coups-Plotters Media about Capriles?

Right, Capriles is "persecuted by the regime", arrested as a "political prisoner"[5]. Sure.

Abusing of his power as Mayor of Baruta, he had his municipal police forces participating in the coup. He actively participated in illegal actions such as blocking a military base[6], creating conditions for teams of snipers to act (to kill civilians[6] at distance) and participating in the attacks[6] and aggressions against Chavistas. Again, the Western MSM and Western governments call him a "political prisoner". Sure.

Western Lying Media constantly crying rivers of crocodile tears for the "oppressed Venezuelans", telling us over and over that criminals like Henrique Capriles or Leopoldo López are victims of state persecution. Surprisingly (or not), during the 2-days regime of Pedro Carmona (2002 coup), leftist deputies, governors, mayors and even ministers were aggressed, humiliated and arrested.

For instance, in the state of Tachira, the house of the governor was invaded and vandalized by the opposition who had lost Tachira in democratic elections to the new governor Ronald Blanco La Cruz (pro-Chávez), who was brutally aggressed and then arrested.

Tarek William Saab, a deputy of the National Assembly was arrested by the criminal opposition. The same happened to Ramón Rodríguez Chacín, Minister of Justice. And so on.

Prostituted Western Media and perverted organizations like Human Rights Watch or Amnesty International saw nothing, investigated nothing, reported nothing, and exposed none of the crimes committed against Chavistas... Shameless Western world!

Capriles Radonsky and his fellow criminal Leopoldo López, during the 2002 coup[7], ordered police forces to invade, loot and vandalize government buildings, the state TV headquarters and many other state institutions, but that's just fine for Western media always selling us these two as brave "freedom fighters".

Meanwhile, police forces following the orders of the coup-plotters massacred 50 pro-Chávez protesters, and injured 400 more, committing the very same crimes they falsely accused Chávez of having committed 2 days before.

In a report[8] published in 2003, shameless Amnesty International (AI) Orwellianly dared to announce the numbers of victims without mentioning wether they were injured or killed by forces involved in the failed coup and by foreign agents with links to the Mossad. Worse, in the same report, Amnesty International shamelessly implied *Círculos Bolivarianos* (pro-government) were behind the violence and attacks on journalists. The very opposite happened and it is well documented. AI smeared the victims and whitewashed the crimes of the opposition. Shameless AI!

During and after the 2002 failed coup, Western prostituted media (specifically the Portuguese prostituted RTP I was watching back then) kept telling us Chávez had massacred many people (lies completely dismantled) and never, never told us anything about the real massacres committed by the coup-plotters surrounded by millions of people asking Chávez to be brought back. Shameless Western MSM, always siding with criminals and with all sorts of illegality...

*

In the previous chapters, I already shared many examples of extreme violence (read "terror attacks"). Undeniable and shocking examples of executions and mass destruction by the opposition are widely available online, for those willing to know the truth, for those rare beings daring to seek the truth.

In Venezuela, thanks to the many millions illegally spent by the US, dozens of groups get the training, the money and the equipment they use to commit all those crimes. There's no room here to describe all the crimes committed by all the criminal groups. But I can share with you a very clear example: the auto-proclaimed Resistencia de Lechería and its terrorist actions. A picture is worth a thousand words; I would add that a video is worth a million words. There's no way to describe those actions. You have to witness those crimes with your own eyes.

Watch it, members of "Resistencia de Lechería" attacking passive police forces with rockets:

Sources 10, 11 – Extremely violent crimes committed by the opposition

Watch this horrendous crime[12], a pro-government citizen, member of the Colectivos, killed by a mortar launched by members of the terrorist group Resistencia de Lechería (the West call them "peaceful opposition" allegedly "oppressed by the regime"!). Later on, the body of their victim was set on fire and, eventually, desecrated!

*

One more example of the horrendous crimes committed by the opposition occurred on April 11, 2017, during another US-sponsor round of coup attempt. On that day, opposition armed gangs attacked the Maternal and Child Health Hospital Hugo Chávez[13]. These opposition criminals set the hospital on fire, with 54 children and newborn babies inside!

165

Yes, 54 children and newborn babies inside, about to be burned alive by the same people Western Lying Media call "oppressed peaceful protesters!"

According to Venezuela's Foreign Minister Delcy Rodriguez[14]:

"We were attacked by violent groups that showered us with stones and sharp objects (and) then burned a large amount of garbage from the hospital — the smoke penetrated inside the premises."

Source 15 - Attack on Hospital Hugo Chávez

For a long period, the hospital had to be protected by members of the Circulos Bolivarianos (*labeled as wild savage criminal leftists* by Western Lying Media) in order to remain open.

Believe it or not, after more than 2 years, the page of this hospital on Wikipedia[16] (in Spanish) doesn't have any information about this crime, proving once again Wikipedia is all but fair or impartial. Wikipedia is incredibly biased. On the same page, there is "information" about the poor conditions felt in the hospital in 2018. Sure, and what about the reasons behind it? What about years of artificially-imposed hyperinflation of prices of medicines and medical equipment? What about the Western sanctions on medicines and medical equipment? Shame on Wikipedia!

*

Beating up pro-Chavistas who don't want to strike; attacking businesses of those who don't want to go on strike; to build barricades to prevent people from going to work; setting fire on the entries of poor neighborhoods so pro-government civilians can't go to work; shooting dead civilians for daring to break the barricades of illegally enforced strikes; provoking accidents with oil and wires put on the barricades, where people die strangled in the wires or in consequence of accidents with their vehicles slipping on oil...

All this has been happening systematically, over the past seven years. All this is scandalously omitted by our pro-terrorists Mainstream Media. Worse, the overwhelming majority of the people killed, who then appeared on the Western MSM "lists of victims of Maduro's oppression", are precisely the victims of these acts of opposition terrorism and of other equally horrendous crimes: people burned alive, killed with rockets while driving vehicles, etc. All Chavistas, of course.

Never the Western Media informed the Western audience (they also don't want to know) about all these acts of terrorism. They never took the side of these many thousands of Chavistas dead or mourning their lost relatives.

And they always call "repression of the regime" to the too mild and peaceful police forces' attempts to put an end to the blatant terrorism. Police and military personnel are killed and wounded in grenade and bomb attacks, in broad daylight, without even fighting back or defending themselves. Yet, for that fundamentalist Western MSM, Maduro "oppresses" and end of the discussion! Sure.

Ultimate irony: when, in the West, genuine strikes are convened and organized by leftist political parties and leftist citizens, the MSM often call them lazy anarchists and *ask* them to go back to work; when wealthy Venezuelans impose "strikes" (by closing their own factories and businesses), while right-wing terrorist organizations commit all the crimes listed above, the very same MSM scream out loud and cry for the right of right-wing Venezuelan millionaires of European descent to enforce strikes recurring to massacres and vandalism, and preventing native Venezuelans and black Venezuelans from exercising their constitutional right to go to work!

Vile arrogant schizophrenic Western World!

*

I'll give you one more example of right-wing terrorism in Venezuela: the Manos Blancas[17] (White Hands), a Venezuelan "students movement" formed in 2007 and funded by US agencies like the Albert Einstein Institute that brought the Serbs Slobodan Dinovicy and Ivan Marovic (Otpor!'s[18] "regime change" experts) to implement Gene Sharp's ideas and plans for Venezuela. The face of the group in

2007 was Yon Goicochea, a specialist in *Sharp* techniques. Manos Blancas are known for their acts of urban violence, but they go much further than that, using psychological war of disinformation and manipulation, and that is precisely what I want you to be aware of.

I want to bring your attention to the fact that there is, in Venezuela, many cases of US interferences sponsoring terrorism disguised as *student and youth insurrections*. Worse, this faked and injected insurrections are then romanticized by Mainstream Media... and westerners swallow it!

Golinger and Allard exhaustively explained how obscure American agents (and of other nationalities) are behind the numerous cases of terrorism disguised as irreverence in Venezuela and in other parts of the world. They also draw attention to the ultimate incoherence: the US administration sponsors dissent abroad, in clear examples of illegal interventionism; at the same time, at home, the US chases down and eliminates any kind of legal dissent against its fascist regime. Here is an excerpt from their book[2]:

The creators of the successful and "super-technological" campaign of Obama joined forces with other agencies in Washington to design the perfect strategy. They combined two new forces in politics - youth and new technologies. It was a combination capable of achieving what for several years had made life difficult for the CIA: [to be able to inject] regime changes in countries that are not subordinate to the interests of the United States, without showing Washington's involvement. The "Manos Blancas" student movement in Venezuela, funded and formed by US agencies, plus the anti-communist protests in Moldova, the demonstrations against the Iranian government and the latest virtual protests against President Chávez are all examples of this new strategy. New technologies like: Twitter, Facebook, YouTube and others are the main weapons, and traditional media, such as CNN and its affiliates, help exaggerate the real impact of these movements by promoting false and distorted opinions about their importance and legitimacy."

Think about it. And read the book USAID, NED y CIA - La agresión permanente[2] if you can read Spanish. If you can't, the content of this book is a powerful reason to motivate you to learn Spanish.

Example of Organized Violence - 2013

Between 14 and 21 of April 2013[19], plenty of public property was destroyed and eleven persons were killed as a result of the so-called "guarimbas" or "arrecheras", words to describe urban violent actions committed by the opposition to destabilize and provoke chaos. These guarimbas were convoked by Henrique Capriles Radonski, who lost the 2012 presidential elections and did not accept the results. Capriles, considered a persecuted hero in the West, had no qualms to invite Venezuelans to burn down the country and kill other fellow Venezuelans supporting the government. And so they did.

The 11 persons killed were all supporters of Maduro's democratically elected government. Some of them were children. The 11 persons[20] were all killed by opposition's terrorists who can't accept democratic results.

Figure 1:

DEADLY VIOLENCE IN VENEZUELA
April 2013

11 | 0

WHO DIED: Pro-government civilians
WHO KILLED: Opposition members

WHO DIED: Opposition members
WHO KILLED: ???????????

On April 14, Luis Eduardo García (24 years old) was shot dead while peacefully protesting with other revolutionary youngsters against Capriles' call for violence. Also on April 14, José Luis Ponce Ordóñez (45 years old), Rosiris Reyes (44 years old) and Johnny

Pacheco (37 years old) were shot with guns, dying later from their injuries. They were protecting a public hospital (Centro de Diagnóstico Integral, in Piedra Azul) under the attack of opposition terrorists.

On April 15, Rey David Chacín González (11 years old) Johan Hernández (22 years old) and María Victoria Báez (12 years old) were killed while peacefully celebrating the triumph of the Bolivarian Revolution. 13 others were injured in the attack. Also on April 15, Gerardo Rico (39 years old) was violently attacked by Capriles' supporter. He died on May 8, in a hospital.

Keler Guevara a police officer (PNB) was shot dead while on duty.

Hender José Bastardo Agreda (21 years old) was shot dead while driving a motorbike. Henry Rangel La Rosa (32 years old) was shot dead while celebrating Maduro's victory right in front of his house.

All these lost lives are worthless for vile Western MSM apologists of savages "regime changes" in Venezuela and elsewhere.

All these lives are worthless for the US and European governments financing Capriles and his fellow criminals!

To prove socialism does not work, the US and some European nations sponsor those who sabotage and destroy the great achievements of the socialist revolution in Venezuela.

Vile West will never change!

The list[19] of public property and public services destroyed during those days is immense, proving the terrorist opposition is not pleased to witness the national wealth being spent to improve the standards of living of those who had nothing under US-allied colonial-minded fascist governments.

The criminal opposition destroyed, vandalized or set on fire at the least:

- 35 buildings of Barrio Adentro, a national social welfare program established by Hugo Chávez;
- 2 hospitals;
- 9 governmental institutions:
- 3 PSUV (Maduro's party) headquarters;
- 3 CNE (National Electoral Council) headquarters;
- Buildings belonging to 18 alternative and communitarian media;
- 39 headquarters of Misión Mercal, PDVAL and Casas de Alimentación, 3 food supply networks created by Hugo Chávez to democratize people's access to food.

Here is some footage showing vandalized infrastructure:

Source 21 – Centro de Diagnóstico Integral de Palo Verde, a hospital for emergency medical services
Source 22 – Several clinics
Source 23 – Community health center in Barinas State
Source 24 - Public buses in Miranda State
Source 25 – Three PSUV headquarters in Barinas, Táchira and Anzoátegui

These are just a few examples of the many crimes committed by the opposition. The list goes on and on.

All these crimes against humanity and against the fundamental rights of Venezuelan human beings are labeled by the Western MSM as "peaceful protests". Am I missing something or, once and for all, should we all start calling them Western Prostituted Media?

In the US and EU, committing such crimes would certainly result in many years of imprisonment.

In Venezuela, *nobody can't be arrested or even stopped*, otherwise perverted and vicious Amnesty Internacional[26] accuses Maduro's government of "excessive use of force", "policy repression" and "crackdown on free speech". So do Western MSM.

But the Venezuelan people who had endured 20 years of endless sabotage, terrorism, and aggression are tired of all this US-sponsored violence. Look what they have to say:

Source 27 – "Nicolás Maduro, we ask you for justice to be done"
Source 28 – "We ask for justice; arrest fascist Henrique Capriles"

But the Western MSM omit and censor this side of the story, silencing the true victims of the conflict.

In the West, prostituted "journalists" and Lying Mainstream Media shamelessly invert the narrative and present the aggressors as victims, in order to convince the Western sheep-like humans to feel empathy towards criminals and terrorists, as they do with the Syrian conflict: "baa..."

They lie ostensibly, they manipulate information about certain events, they recycle footage from different conflicts, they omit essential information, and so on.

All this was done in 2013 to divert the Western populace's attention away from the opposition's attempt to reenact the 2002 failed coup. In 2002, the US and Venezuelan white elite didn't manage to corrupt Chávez, so they tried to force him out. In 2013 Chávez was already dead. Maduro (unfortunately for the imperial US) won the presidential elections, so the only option for the US rogue state was to do more of the same: another coup attempt.

Again failed, but not the last one. They have been trying over and over. The last attempt occurred only 1 month ago, on April 30, 2019.

In the 2013 failed coup, the idea was to generate generalized chaos from April 14 on: after the results of the presidential elections (Nicolás Maduro won, Henrique Capriles lost). Capriles and his party had already planned to not recognize Maduro's victory. They knew in advance they would not win, and they decided in advance they would react violently. These are the guys European MSM label as "oppressed" by the "regime"!

With violence and chaos widespread, a psychological and mediatic campaign would be implemented to make people question the results of the last elections (the same kind of injected violence implemented in 2002 to make people question the legitimacy of Chávez's government). That would temporarily (or permanently) discredit

Maduro's public image (as happened to Chávez's public image in 2002), open the door for a coup attempt or a civil war (like in 2002). If necessary, the US Army was ready to intervene militarily (as it was in 2002) and fully implement the latest dictatorship in what the US administration calls its "backyard".

The Venezuelan Intelligence Service (SEBIN), since at the least October 2012, was investigating the people behind the destabilizing plan for the upcoming elections and known by its creators as plan Conexión Abril. Behind this plan to provoke chaos as a way to implement a "regime change" coup, among others, were Raúl Isaías Baduel (former Minister of Defense) and Antonio Rivero (leader of Voluntad Popular, one of those groups funded by the US). Antonio Rivero has links to other US-sponsored groups of "youth insurgence" such as Juventud Activa Venezolana Unida, Movimiento 13 or Operación Libertad.

On June 5, 2013, after being arrested by the SEBIN and accused of being involved in the preparation of this failed coup, a US citizen named Tracy Timothy Hallet[29] (35 years old, born in Michigan) was forced to leave Venezuela. If Venezuela were a dictatorship like Pinochet's Chile or a terrorist rogue state like the US (I am thinking about Guantanamo, Abu Ghraib and other US chambers of terror), Tracy Timothy Hallet would have been harshly tortured and, eventually, killed. But Venezuela is not, no matter what Western sheep-like humans believe in!

*

While in the parallel reality made up by Western MSM "people are oppressed by Maduro's dictatorship", in the real world, politicians, police forces, military forces and humble civilians (often dark-skinned) who voted for the democratically elected President Maduro are systematically purged. The assassinations and acts of lynching of pro-Chavistas are continuously committed in pure mafia style.

But let the US-sponsored right-wing organizations commit mafia-like crimes, otherwise prostituted journalists would go wild on Venezuela, right?

For those willing to follow real reality and not made-up *realities,* there are always alternatives, such as Telesur English. In Telesur[30] there are coherent human beings reporting what is censored by Western MSM:

"Western mainstream media outlets have remained silent regarding the violence waged against government supporters, left-wing activists and public servants, which many believe is an attempt to undermine the future of the Chavista movement in the country."

This Venezuelan state-funded news channel (yes, state-funded, so what?) often offers detailed lists of victims of the many campaigns of terror waged by the terrorist opposition. If Western MSM have something to say about those lists, please go on! Tell us what is wrong with the lists (full of pro-government victims).

And if there's nothing wrong with the lists, why don't Western Media share them with the Western public?

And if there's nothing wrong with the lists, why do Western Media keep accusing Maduro of crimes actually committed by the opposition against Maduro's supporters and even police forces?

And why don't westerners pose themselves these kinds of questions?

Probably because most of them have lost the ability to reason!

Probably because they prefer to listen arrogantly ignorant persons like the unprofessional Jorge Ramos[31] disrespecting Maduro and rudely throwing lists of criminals in his face[32]:

Probably because they prefer to believe in fabricated "oppression" in Venezuela, instead of acknowledging real oppression nearby, in Honduras, a country whose freedom was stolen 10 years ago by an illegal US-backed military coup[33].

In Honduras, the US removed the democratically elected President Zelaya and imposed unwanted capitalism, oppression, and hunger, the reason why there are caravans of Hondurans (and not of Venezuelans) walking towards the US soil.

In Honduras, there are real and massive protests [34, 35, 36] against the government, systematically and violently repressed by the polices forces[37]. But westerners don't want to hear about these real protests[38, 39]. They only want to *know* about the Western-fabricated ones in Venezuela.

In Honduras, there are people ready to fight against the US-imposed right-wing dictatorship. They are tired of it. They are outraged. And they know how to show their outrage[40]:

Sources 41, 42 – US Embassy in Tegucigalpa set on fire

Yes, yes, Hondurans setting US Embassy on fire. Well done, for two reasons. First, the US violated International Law and Hondurans' rights when they militarily imposed a dictatorial regime; therefore, don't expect Hondurans to respect the International Law that is supposed to protect the integrity of the US Embassy in Tegucigalpa.

Yet, during 10 years of imposed regime, Hondurans didn't attack it, and here I move to the second reason: a few days ago the US invaded Venezuelan Embassy in Washington, in blatant disrespect for Venezuelan sovereignty and the International Law; the US opened a Pandora Box of violated embassies... from now on, dear not dear US administration, get used watching your embassies being assaulted, destroyed or burned down.

I will applaud each time it happens. And, believe me, I will not be the only one applauding... millions of revolutionary minds all over the world will applaud and celebrate symbolic attacks against US Terror State.

Many more US embassies will burn and they must burn, burned down until nothing is left. The US rogue state invites the people of the world to do so. The US Terror State only understands the language of terror, so with terror shall be treated.

The US rogue state created the 8 years-long war in Syria. The US illegally occupies one-third of Syrian territory. The US bombs factories of medicines and sponsors terrorist organizations in Syria. While stealing Syrian oil, the US imposes an energy embargo on Syria. As if it was not enough, now, the US Terror State bombs[43, 44] boats transporting Syrian oil in Syrian territory to be consumed by the Syrian people.

What else? What kind of terrorist action has the US to commit in order to wake up the minds of those westerners who have lost the ability to reason?

Leopoldo López - The Hero of Western MSM

For Western MSM Leopoldo López is a "freedom fighter" persecuted by the "regime" who has him as a "political prisoner". The Western MSM praise amazing deeds he never did, while forgetting all his crimes that, if committed in the US and other countries, would have led him to a life spent in a high-security prison: participation in coup attempts, calls for violent uprising days after democratic elections lost to Maduro and unanimously recognized as fair by plenty of international observers, etc.

Somehow, the Western MSM manage to miss all the dark facts about Leopoldo López, as if their journalists were all blind, deaf, mentally retarded and had no access to the internet, Venezuelan state and communitarian media, flights to and from Venezuela, and dictionaries Spanish-English-Spanish.

Some prostituted media, as the Portuguese state channel RTP, go as far as inviting Leopoldo López's father to invert reality affirming unproven bullshit like "80% of the Venezuelans support Guaidó" on prime time.

In Western MSM, objectivity and facts have no value. Nowadays, to announce live on prime time, that "the sky is green" is enough for the sky to become green. Attempts to reimplement objective reality are a waste of time, given the "safe space" shields and all the other postmodern shields in vogue.

Western politicians are going wild too. Someone in the Spanish Popular Party decided to invite Leopoldo López Gil[45], father of Leopoldo López, to be a candidate in the European parliamentary elections. Shamelessly, the EU has been interfering in Venezuelan internal affairs for ages. To make things easier for the Venezuelan criminal opposition, now they have Leopoldo López Gil in Brussels, as close as possible from their European bosses. Lovely.

But let's go back to Leopoldo López, the convicted criminal who called for a violent uprising against Maduro's presidential victory, as he, Leopoldo López, was not willing "to wait 6 more years to be heard". Usually, all over the world, defeated candidates feel like not willing to wait some more years to be heard. But that's the first rule of the democratic game, you dumb López: you have to wait! If you do not want to play by the rules and prefer to call for the violent overthrow of a man elected a few days before, well, in that case, prepare your bag because the police will be soon knocking at your door.

Source 46 - Sad Leopoldo López, sad Guaidó and the policemen who sided with their failed coup, 30.04.2019

I could write pages about López's past crimes, but I will not. In 2014, the book *Venezuela se Respecta*[47] offered some interesting glimpses about his dark past:

'Leopoldo López's record includes his active participation in the events that led to the coup d'état against President Hugo Chávez in April 2002. López, who by that time was mayor of the opulent municipality of Chacao, east of Caracas, took advantage of his authority to start a hunt for Chavista leaders, including the Minister of the Interior of Chávez, Ramón Rodríguez Chacín, and the revolutionary deputy Tarek William Saab, who were arrested the day after the coup by officers of the Police of Chacao led by Leopoldo López.

In a television interview broadcasted on April 12, López confessed having led an operation that consisted of employing officers of the Chacao police to strip drivers of their keys and to cross their cars in a way that would prevent the departure of troops and prevent the tank battalion loyal to President Chávez from reaching Caracas.

Leopoldo López's conspiracy past includes his active participation in the violent protests of the so-called Plan Guarimba, in 2004. He also ignored the results of the recall referendum that favored President Chávez in 2004.

It was this man who first called to the insurrectional plan currently being implemented against the democratic government of Venezuela, with his appeal made on January 23th for people to remain in the streets until the overthrow of President Nicolás Maduro. 'Venezuelans are obliged to demand the departure of a corrupt government'."

Example of Organized Violence - 2014

The call for these 6 months of violence, destruction, and assassinations was made by the criminal María Corina Machado and the criminal (or "political prisoner", in *Westernish*) Leopoldo López. These two went to the streets calling for a violent uprising that should last until Maduro would resign ("la salida", "the exit" in English, as they decided to call the coup attempt).

These were working on behalf of the US administration that was pushing all the opposition forces (heavily sponsored by the US administration) to stick together to finally achieve Yankee's long ambition: to end with socialist Venezuela. The name of Leopoldo López is cited in US diplomatic documents at the least 77 times. Learn more about it in the article *What the Wikileaks Cables Say about Leopoldo López*[48].

María Corina Machado worked in close collaboration with several other coup-plotters, including the US Ambassador to Venezuela William Brownfield and US Ambassador to Colombia Kevin Whitaker. Other active participants of this US-sponsored attempt to "regime change" were the powerful Gustavo Tarre, Ricardo Koesling, Henrique Romer, Robert Alonso, Diego Arria, etc. Leaked conversations between these and other individuals leave no room for doubts about the clear plan to remove Maduro and the clear plan to make Venezuela suffer and burn as a way to get Maduro removed.

Here are so examples of leaked emails[47] exchanged between Corina Machado and other fellow coup-plotters:

- **Corina Machado to Henrique Romer:** "With this support, that of the European Parliament, the State [USA] and the American Senate [USA] doing what was promised, the international lobby is at its best since the beginning of the fight."
"That being the case, we will continue to encourage the agitation of all young people, and especially students, with these efforts."

- **Corina Machado to Gustavo Tarre:** "Kevin Whitaker [US Ambassador to Colombia] has already reconfirmed his support and indicated the new steps. We have a checkbook stronger than that of the regime, to break the international safety ring (...)."
- **Corina Machado to Gustavo Tarre:** "Streets, more ungovernability, the action of activists in the Metro [subway], Metrobus, Bolivarian high schools, public universities, everything, we will invade (...)."
- **Corina Machado to Diego Arria:** "We have to clean up this mess, starting with the head, taking advantage of the global situation with Ukraine and now Thailand, the sooner the better."
- **Corina Machado to Diego Arria:** "(...) I think the time has come to join efforts, make the necessary calls and get the funding to annihilate Maduro and the rest will fall by itself."
- **Burelli Pedro Mario to Diego Arria:** "(...) we go for everything and with everything, against everything. We have the [US State] Department, the [US] embassy, and now the [US] Senate sanctions are coming."
- **Burelli Pedro Mario to Diego Arria:** "Let's take the streets of the country, including the [presidential] palace streets, as we should, and encircle that son of a bitch. We have people in Miraflores thanks to friend Bocaranda, every step will be useful when the time comes."
- **Ricardo Koesling sent an image to Roberto Alonso**, in which we can see Maduro's portrait used as a shooting target[49].

This messages exchanged by the opposition leave no room for doubt: they work with foreign agents, they admittedly follow US orders, they call for the destruction of public property (schools, subway, universities, etc.), they call for the death of their elected president, they admit being funded by Western governments, they prove to be behind the 2014 pre-planned uprising, etc.

Westerners don't know what it's going on in Venezuela because they do not want to know and because they have lost the ability to reason!

*

Source 50 - A "peaceful protester" supposedly "repressed" by the "regime"

The victims - During this period of extreme violence convened by the Venezuela opposition and sponsored with US dollars, 43 persons died and 878 suffered injuries.

In this article, you can find a list of 41 of them, with detailed information about each victim, including photographies: *Conozca los 41 fallecidos por las protestas violentas opositoras en Venezuela: La mayoría son víctimas de barricadas*[51].

Figure 2:

DEADLY VIOLENCE IN VENEZUELA
January 2014 to June 2014

35 | 8

81,4% of total (43)	18,6% of total (43)
WHO DIED: Pro-government civilians, police forces, opposition members	WHO DIED: Opposition members
WHO KILLED: Opposition members	WHO KILLED: Police Forces

43 people died[52], 35 of whom were killed by violent groups of the Venezuelan opposition, while 8 people died as a result of possible disproportionate use of force by the police forces.

Even if the policemen who killed 8 people while on duty... while defending public property and the safety of all those aggressed by the violent opposition, were all found guilty of having committed murder, anyway, their fatal "crimes" correspond to 18,6% of the total. The other 81,4% were committed by the opposition. Knowing the violence had been convened by the leaders of the opposition and by the US/EU interference, how can someone possibly blame Maduro's government for all the deaths and violence that took place during those 5 months?

Well, it's easy, prostituted journalists and prostituted members of AI and HRW only have to turn off rational thinking (if they still have it). And so do most of them. For weeks, the covers of virtually all Western newspapers offered shocking and manipulative titles, constantly *reminding* us "Maduro was massacring its people"...

Maduro orders massacres, white is black, war is peace and the sky is green, right?

*

Let's now talk about the destruction, clearly done by the opposition and not by the police forces. The Western MSM don't like so much this topic, as it is much harder to manipulate it and accuse the polices forces (of a socialist nation) of having destroyed plenty of public property used for social purposes, right?

Caracas Subway- The criminal opposition surely doesn't like public services. One of its main targets was the subway system of Caracas, mainly used by low-income classes. The criminal opposition damaged 6 trains (three of Line 2 and three of Line 3) and 10 subway stations, destroying escalators, CCTV cameras, gates, fire systems, windows, furniture, etc. Other 95 units of Metrobus were damage. The Metrobus Operations Center in Altamira Square was burned down and destroyed. Twelve Metrobus routes were affected by the violent attacks known as "guarimbas". 200 users and 40 employees were injured. Subway stations in many rich areas are constantly besieged.

National Power Grid - Two regional headquarters were attacked in Carabobo State. 23 vehicles damaged all over the country. Attempted sabotage in 2 electric substations (Los Olivos and San Cristóbal).

CANTV, the state-run telephone and internet provider -
One telephone exchange was destroyed and seven vehicles were burned in Morán, Lara State. Communication tower vandalized in Barquisimeto, Lara State. Two trucks with mobile communications equipment attacked in Maracaibo, Zulia State. A customer service office attacked in Santa Elena, Lara State. A radio station attacked in Caracas.

These are just a few examples of the many crimes committed by the opposition. The list goes on[52] and on[53] and on[54] and on[55]. Universities, governmental buildings, sports facilities, public hospitals vandalized and destroyed. Dozens of tons of food of social aid burned. 5000 trees cut down, 30 hectares in Warairarepano National burned down. Everything is allowed. The criminal and terrorist opposition in Venezuela could drop an atomic bomb over Brussels or Washington, and yet, the US and European politicians and journalists would continue to call them "peaceful protesters, persecuted victims of Maduro's regime".

Here is some footage of their terrorist attacks on public infrastructure:

Source 56 – Public property destroyed
Source 57 – Supreme Court destroyed
Sources 58, 59 – Public University UNEFA burned down

I could share here hundreds of pictures and links, but it is all freely available online, and the examples of Western-paid terror in Venezuela are almost endless. Search it yourself. It is very easy.

As you can clearly see in the available footage, terrorist opposition of European descent can't stand watching the money made with Venezuelan resources being spent to create public buses, public hospitals, public schools or public universities with which the *others* can finally cease to be poor, sick and uneducated. The ultra-racist and supremacist castes of European descent can't stand watching the liberation of their dark-skinned slaves; they can't watch their slaves of the last 5 centuries being well-fed, healthy and educated.

That's why Capriles and López are wrong and Maduro is right. That's why Guaidó is backed by the mightiest war machine humankind ever saw, while Maduro is backed by the majority of the Venezuelan people. That's why, one month later, Leopoldo López was finally arrested[60]!

That's why Western sheep-like humans are wrong about Venezuela. They find it reasonable to protest, week after week, in France, for an even better social welfare state (Yellow Vests and friends) but, most of them, are against those building a (better) social state in Venezuela, and they side with the imperial warmongers in Washington. "Baa..."

*

To be convincing, and knowing they are lying, Venezuelan private media, Western MSM and their fellow social-media trolls need to use dirty tactics such as recycling footage then showed as *pieces of evidence* of their lies. "Images from Syria, Egypt, Brazil, Spain, Chile, Colombia and other countries have been recycled by newspapers and digital media to fraudulently depict Venezuela's conflict[53]."

And so, a pro-independence protest in Catalonia becomes a demonstration against Maduro[61].

A religious event becomes a demonstration against the government[62].

Events in Argentina and Spain become events in Venezuela[63].

On February 26, 2014, a Spanish *journalist* named "Alfonso Merlos", working for the Spanish newspaper La Razón ("the sixth-highest circulation among general-interest Spanish dailies"[64]), twitted a set of pictures showing a woman seriously injured. According to his tweet (later removed), the woman was a victim of the "Venezuelan extreme-left government"[65].

He was lying[66], of course. The pictures had been uploaded on Instagram, one day before, by a US citizen named Gabriella, who decided to show the injuries inflicted on her by her boyfriend.

Read *Girl Badly Beaten By Boyfriend Shares Her Story & Photos Of Her Injury*[67].

Two days before Alfonso Merlos' lies, a Venezuelan man died in Pueblo Nuevo. According to North American, European, South American (Brazil included[68]) and Venezuelan private media outlets selling us another coup attempt in Venezuela, the 33 years old man had been shot dead by Bolivarian National Guard forces firing buckshot pellets (among other also false versions).

Again, they were lying[69]. The man died in the building he was assaulting with other fellow thugs when he lost balance and fell from a high height. Nobody shot anything against him; there were no police forces throwing tear gas on his direction; nobody touched him[70].

And so on; search for the rest. As you can conclude, everything is permitted when it comes to smear democratic socialism.

Example of Organized Violence - 2017

Like in 2013 and 2014, violent protests, looting, and opposition-organized uprising resulted in enormous destruction and death. From April 6th until July 27th, at the least 131 persons died. The Western Mainstream Media, as always, blamed Maduro. As always, they were lying.

The story is basically the same as in 2013 and 2014, but with a higher number of deadly fatalities. If you want to learn more about the victims of 2007 uprising, you can check these 4 detailed lists (3 articles and one documentary). The articles and the documentary present different numbers, but it is no mistake, they just cover different periods of time and the data was still being collected at the time some of the lists were published:

List 1 - 95 deaths from April 6th to July 1st (documentary by Abby Martin)[71]
List 2 - 107 deaths from April 6th to June 30th (aporrea.org)[72]
List 3 - 124 deaths from April 6th to July ? (telesurenglish.net)[73]
List 4 - 131 deaths from April 6th to July 27th (albaciudad.org)[74]

These lists are more comprehensive than previous ones and provide detailed information about the victims and the murderers. Instead of just informing if the victim was pro-government or anti-government, these lists explain if the persons killed were protesting or not, how were they killed, if they could be identified with one of the sides or not, etc. There's also information about the police officers who killed anti-government protesters while on duty and fighting murderous uprising. The Venezuelan government gave the names of the police officers arrested and waiting for trial, proving how open and democratic is Venezuela.

Telesur English produced an excellent infographic about the victims[75]. I highly recommend a careful analysis of it.

Let's see what the numbers tell us:

- Only 5 of the 124 victims were killed by polices officers.

- 5 of the victims were police officers.
- 12 victims could be clearly identified as Chavistas (pro-government).
- 30 were bystanders, victims of opposition violence.
- 49 were killed in the protesters, victims of opposition's violence or accidental deaths of those protesting violently.
- 10 were killed in the barricades created by the violent opposition to block Chavistas.
- 13 were killed during the acts of looting perpetrated by the opposition, victims of opposition's violence or accidental deaths of those looting.

So, in 124 deaths, we have 5 police officers (4%) killed by the opposition, 5 members of the opposition (4%) killed by the police and 114 deaths (92%) caused by opposition's violence (pro-government, unknown, neutral or opposition members).

In 124, we have 5 persons (4%) killed by the police and 119 persons (96%) killed as the result of opposition's violence. How can we possibly blame Maduro's government for the deaths, violence, and destruction that occurred in 2017?

Figure 3:

DEADLY VIOLENCE IN VENEZUELA
April 2017 to July 2017

119 | 5

96% of total (124)   4% of total (124)

WHO DIED: Pro-government civilians, police forces, opposition members, unknown/neutral

WHO KILLED: Opposition members

WHO DIED: Opposition members

WHO KILLED: Police Forces

We can't blame the Venezuelan government for the deaths caused by a criminal opposition that doesn't respect democratic results and convene violent actions. Even the 5 persons killed by the police forces, those deaths occurred in a context of organized criminality destroying public property and killing innocent civilians, as would have happened in Germany, in the US or in Japan!

Yet, according to Western Lying media and their manipulative narrative, Maduro's government and only Maduro's government is to be blamed, no matter how many millions of US dollars were behind it; no matter how well armed with grenades and explosives was the criminal opposition; no matter how many hospitals, universities, buses and tons of food were vandalized, destroyed or burned by the criminal opposition.

The West is blind because the West wants to be blind and because the West is (also) guilty of all this violence.

*

In 2019, several Venezuelans died as a direct consequence of this last *coup season*. Always the same sad and unnecessary story.

It is time for westerners to open their eyes and prevent their criminal governments from supporting the slow-motion genocide inflicted upon the brave Venezuelan people. If not, soon the world would be irreversibly divided into 2 blocks. Venezuela and other bullied nations like China, Russia, Iran or Syria will prevail and will be in the right block and on the right side of history. Westerners won't.

INTERNATIONAL COMMUNITY
07.06.2019

How many times a day is the expression "international community" pronounced on Western Mainstream Media in a completely dishonest manner? How many times is this expression used by Western MSM to refer only to the US and its Western client states?

Too many times. Too often.

If one takes the time to compare enough Western news and reports, the conclusion is simple and obvious. In Western MSM *newspeak,* "International community" means:

- USA, Canada, Europe, Israel, Australia, New Zealand, Japan, and South Korea.
- Sometimes it also includes parts of South America and a few other obedient US client states.

A map with the countries that do not recognize the State of Palestine shown in grey, and the countries that recognize the State of Palestine shown in green, is a perfect illustration of the Western concept of "international community":

Source 1 – World map with the countries that recognize the State of Palestine

In conclusion, the manipulated and manipulative concept of "international community" we constantly hear on Western MSM refers to 30-50 countries in a world where the UN recognizes 193 as sovereign nations. The math is definitely wrong.

And what about semantics? According to the Oxford Dictionary[2]:

"The international community: [phrase] the countries of the world considered collectively."

Interesting, the world considered collectively, not partially. I definitely agree with the definition provided by the Oxford Dictionary, but most of the Western journalists, by incompetence, brainlessness or obedience, do not seem to agree.

It is very common to read and hear Western MSM journalists affirming the "international community" condemns Palestinians for having launched rockets against Israel, forgetting that most of the countries actually condemn the occupation of Palestine by the Zionist apartheid regime.

Worse, the same Western MSM journalists tend to omit the fact that, when the UN Assembly is invited to vote on Palestine-Israel issues, systematically, the US and Israel vote in favor of Israel, a few abstain, and almost all the other countries vote in favor of Palestine. On those occasions, it would be approximately correct to use the expression "international community". But in those precise occasions, Western MSM tend to remain silent.

According to biased and Orwellian Western MSM, the "international community" considers "Assad a criminal", accuses Maduro of "oppressing its people", condemns China for its "invasion of Africa", sees Russia as an "expansionist nation", etc. But in all those examples of mediatic manipulation of reality, "international community" refers to a group of nations that, combined, have a smaller population than China alone!

I insist, in the case of manipulative condemnations against oppressed Palestine for daring to resist Zionist apartheid, and knowing both China and India recognize Palestine, the twisted version of "international community" refers to a number of people smaller than the Indian (1.339 billion) or Chinese (1.386 billion) population, two countries that do recognize both Palestine! Can't you see Western supremacist ideology right here?

If one wants to apply the expression "international community" to a set of countries instead of all "countries of the world considered collectively", the first option should not be the US plus its richer client states, but rather the Non-Aligned Movement (NAM). The Non-Aligned Movement counts with 125 members and Nicólas Maduro is the current Secretary-General. Yes, Nicólas Maduro, the President of Venezuela!

125 countries are more "international community" than the US plus 30 or 40 vassal states without independent foreign policies. With countries like India, Indonesia, Vietnam, Mexico, Nigeria, Egypt, Bangladesh or Pakistan as full members, and China or Brazil with observer status, NAM represents the overwhelming majority of human beings, many victims of crimes, enslavement and plunder committed by the Western World that labels itself as "international community".

My conclusion is that the problem with the Western definition of "international community" has nothing to do with maths or semantics. It has to do with exceptionalism, racism, and supremacism. The supremacist westerners, used to see as sub-humans all the Africans, Asians and Native Americans they raped, tortured, killed and enslaved (and continue to enslave and kill with economic neocolonialism), can't possibly accept to include those nations in the concept of "international community", a concept born from a Western perspective of deep civilizational exceptionalism and racial supremacism.

*

Supposedly, in that weird parallel reality most westerners live in, Guaidó should be seen (at the least by westerners) as the real President of Venezuela, the less pathetic *argument* being: a few dozen US vassal states plus some fascist regimes in South America say so!

Well, nonsense! The only international organism entitled to recognize (or not) governments of sovereign nations is the UN. All those nations illogically recognizing a non-elected non-candidate as President of Venezuela are governed by morons who don't even understand International Law. If they are not happy with the decision Venezuelans made in May 2018 (when they elected Maduro), they can always complain, somehow, pathetically, during a UN assembly.

They can propose some pathetic measures to force Maduro out of Venezuela´s presidency. Please, go on. The majority of nations on Earth are with Venezuela, so nothing will be changed (and by the way, Russia and China have veto power to block nonsensical crap of that kind).

The UN recognized May 2018 presidential elections as clean and fair elections. So did OAS, whose majority of members, now, following US orders, illogically recognize non-elected Guaidó as the President of Venezuela. If those few dozens of US client states in Europe, South America, and East Asia are not happy with the way things are done at the UN or how the International Law works, they have a very easy solution for their problem: leave the UN, stop abiding by International Law and become rogue states! *Voilà!*

*

As all Western MSM, Wikipedia[3] is also a fan of data manipulation as an efficient tool of propaganda and brainwashing:

Source 4 – World map with the countries that recognize Guaidó or Maduro

Did you notice something strange on the map? Yes, the countries in blue are roughly the so-called "international community" plus the South American fascist regimes, but that's not strange.

According to Wikipedia, the light grey means "no statement", the dark grey "neutral" and the red is used for the nations supporting Maduro. This intentional misinterpretation of data leads to naive or unattentive human beings believing Maduro has less international support than Guaidó. Wrong, wrong and wrong.

Only 2 colors are possible: blue for those nations that, despite being UN members, opt not to recognize the government of a UN member despite the fact the government in question is recognized by the UN. Cognitive dissonance, post-modern opinions, mental retardedness? I don't know and I don't even care about the reasons behind their illogical behavior. Let them be.

All the other nations that show support to Maduro, do support Maduro.

All the other nations saying nothing about, by default, recognize Maduro, as they can't possibly recognize other than the one the UN recognizes.

All the other nations that affirmed to be neutral in the dispute between Venezuela sovereignty and US illegal interference (whose current face is Guaidó), probably do so fearing US sanctions or US embargoes or US bombs. Nevertheless, if they affirm to be neutral in this latest US aggression on Venezuela, as UN members, they will also continue to recognize, by default, the one the UN recognizes.

In conclusion, Wikipedia manipulates data to produce a lie! There are countries recognizing non-elected Guaidó, but they are a tiny minority (in blue). There are other countries abiding by International Law, respecting Venezuela sovereignty and therefore recognizing Maduro's government. These (all the other colors) are the vast majority and represent the overwhelming majority of human beings alive!

As Robin Monotti Graziadei pointed out in a very clearly, 44 countries[5] (23%) recognized Guaidó. Consequently, 149 countries (77%) did not recognize Guaidó. The vast majority of nations on Earth stand for the legality and for Venezuelan sovereignty[6].

*

Let's check and analyze some examples of international support for Maduro's government, almost all of them Machiavellianly omitted or censored by Western MSM for not fitting the fake official *truth* imposed in the West.

African Union - The African Union has 55 members, more than all the members of the hypocritical Western concept of "international community" combined. With an official statement, the African Union, representing 1,2 billion human beings, expressed its support for President Nicolás Maduro. As the Venezuelan Foreign Ministry informed[7] on January 31th, 2019:

"Deputy Chairperson of the African Union, Thomas Kwesi Quartey, has sent a message of solidarity with the people of Venezuela and of support for constitutional President Nicolás Maduro."

1,2 billion people officially supporting Maduro and US/European MSM ignore it?

1,2 billion people officially supporting Maduro and Western MSM keep saying the "international community" (read, as Oxford Dictionary invites: "the countries of the world considered collectively") condemns Maduro for things he didn't do? What does all this mean? Isn't Africa part of the World? Aren't citizens of African nations as human beings as their Western counterparts? What is wrong with the West?

I tell you what is wrong with the West: racism, supremacism and several other *isms*.

In this twisted and utterly sickening Western view of the world: *Africans do not count as people because they are black and lazy; Asians do not count as people because Asian men look like women and the Asian women are better fitted for sexual slavery in Pattaya or Bali; Native Americans do not count as people and so we keep them in natural zoos; the rulers (of our European caste) in Latin America are there to follow our orders, not to open their mouths.*

In that twisted reality sure, no doubt the so-called "international community", the few left from a very racist purge, together, are indeed an international community. Congratulations!

*

A few more examples of countries supporting the democratically elected government of Venezuela and President Maduro:

Chad and Serbia - On March 1st, 2019, President Nicolás Maduro met with Chadian Ambassador Ngote Gali Koutou and with Serbian Ambassador Danilo Pantovic[8].

Iran - Iranians showing support for Venezuelan during a rally backing the Islamic Revolution on its 40th anniversary[9].

Greece - Protesters in the streets of Athens denouncing the alleged unrest in Venezuela as being a US-backed plan to overthrow Maduro[10].

Palestine - Palestinians waving Venezuelan flags in solidarity to Venezuela, a country also victim of Western aggression[11].

Syria - Refugees victims of the 8 years-long Western terror war on Syria showing their support for Maduro in front of the Venezuelan Embassy in Damascus[12].

Uruguay - Tabaré Vázquez, the President of Uruguay, declared to be against US interventionism in Venezuela, despite the fact Mike Pence had asked him to recognize Guaidó as President of Venezuela[13].

Lebanon - Michel Aoun, the President of Lebanon, met the Venezuelan Foreign Minister Jorge Arreaza, reaffirming his country's support for Venezuela[14].

China - Unlike what Wikipedia affirms in its list of countries supporting Guaidó, China clearly didn't distance itself from Maduro's government. On the contrary, China is the most committed country in delivering humanitarian[15] aid to Venezuela to counter the Western genocidal embargo. China deployed a military mission[16] to Venezuela and sent Zhao Bentang, Director General for Latin America of the Ministry of Foreign Affairs, to meet Maduro in Caracas[17].

Russia - Maria Zhakarova and Sergei Lavrov have consistently reassured Russian strong support for the legitimate government of Venezuela and constantly criticized the US administration for the illegal nature of its interference in Venezuelan internal affairs: Read what Lavrov said[18] on May 1st, 2019, in reaction to the failed coup attempt on April 30th:

"It was indicated that the continuation of aggressive steps is fraught with the most serious consequences. Only the Venezuelan people have the right to determine their destiny, for which dialogue between all political forces in the country is

needed, and for which the government has long called for. Destructive pressure from outside, especially force, has nothing to do with the democratic process."

No matter what Guaidó says or believes[19], denying or not the existence of Russian and Chinese support for democratically elected Maduro, the real reality is still there! If he is in denial, let him be. Anyways, his opinions or interpretations of reality are objectively worthless:

"They [Maduro's government] do not have any international allies; it is not true that Russia and China are with them. That's a great fallacy. No one is with them."

Well, the new non-aligned block[20], in a world divided into 2 blocks by Western-imposed choice, is becoming a reality. Delusional members of the Venezuelan "opposition" (like Guaidó) having mental troubles and the US stubbornness on pursuing with their crimes against Venezuela not only will not prevent the new non-aligned block from growing bigger and stronger but are actually speeding it up! History didn't end!

JUAN GUAIDÓ, THE PUPPET

12.06.2019

Guaidó According to the Venezuelan People

First of all, a US puppet with no real career in real politics (violent uprising against a democratic system does not qualify as "doing politics") can't possibly be taken seriously. And so he was not taken seriously by the Venezuelan population. Worse. At the moment he self-proclaimed his person "President of Venezuela", without even having participated in democratic elections (not even a candidate!), 81% of Venezuelans didn't know he existed[1]!

Second, thanks to 20 years of Bolivarianism, spreading knowledge and free access to information about people's own rights, it is too late for the US Empire to inject its dirty puppets in Venezuela. People there know their constitutional rights. They know how the democratic system is supposed to function. They are deeply committed and ready to protect the admirable democratic system they have, the reason why they don't swallow US illegal interventionism and have the right answer ready to be pronounced: "We didn't vote for you, Guaidó. We're not a North American colony."[2]

Third, despite the fact that Guaidó is highly unpopular in Venezuela (I know, Western MSM say the opposite, as they were sure about Saddam's WMD which didn't exist), this traitor insists on moving around in the streets of Caracas, eventually meeting not so kind Venezuelans who (rightly) despise traitors. Thankfully, for Guaidó, Venezuela is a very democratic society (and not the "oppressive regime" he calls it) in which traitors are protected by the police (and not beaten or tortured like in Chile's Pinochet). In democratic Venezuela, Guaidó can announce his readiness to sell his country to the US and call for illegal US military intervention (although 86% of Venezuelans oppose US military intervention[3]) and end the day saved by the "oppressive" police forces working for the "regime."[4]

Fourth, given his unpopularity and the fact he openly proposes to sell his country to the terrorist US, soon or later he would face Venezuelan journalists trapping him with his own illegal and silly acts. On April 30th, Guaidó led the pathetic attack against La

Carlota airbase recurring   to US-made   and   European-made weapons[5] and... Bananas. Yes, bananas[6].

A few days ago, a brave Venezuelan journalist ironically asked him about the *banana* coup[7]. *Poor* Guaidó, visibly embarrassed, and didn't know what to say.

Fifth, besides Guaidó himself, Guaidó's "revolution" was also not popular at all among Venezuelans. Compare[8] the few hundred supporters around him or near the airbase, during the attempted coup (April 30th to May 1st), with the immense crowds supporting Maduro's government on May 1st.

The footage widely available shows the support to Guaidó is very small[9]. The footage widely available shows the support to Maduro is immense[10]. Facts are facts, no matter how much Western MSM cook Guaidó's figures and censor Maduro's figures.

Sixth, he was even not a candidate[11] during the last presidential elections, let alone a winner. Of course, the people of Venezuela can't see him as their president!

Seventh, the Venezuelan people saw many temporary US pawns passing by and know Guaidó will have the same place in history as the others had: the rubbish bin of history! Guaidó is a disposable pawn, of course! As always! Guaidó is taken so not seriously by his Yankee's bosses that apparently his bosses already discarded him.

After having admitted his desire to be President of Venezuela was premature[12] (Call it premature man, in the last time elections held you were even not a candidate!), leaked audio proves Pompeo and the US administration are already planning to find another puppet to steal Maduro's seat.

According to pathetic Pompeo[13], the problem will be to find the right candidate to become the President of Venezuela after the odd success of an illegal US intervention to remove Maduro. *Poor* him, apparently he doesn't know what to do with the forty plus opposition vultures the US keeps feeding in its cradle of potential coup-plotters.

And think about: is it normal? Is it normal to hear the US Secretary of State Mike Pompeo admitting US grotesque interference in Venezuelan internal affairs[14]? The US administration talks about it as if it was not a crime according to International Law. Pompeo, Trump, US former Embassy to the UN Nikky Halley, etc. Shamelessly and openly, they all talk about military intervention. They arrogantly talk about removing Maduro and about selecting the next dictator they would use to once again enslave Venezuelans and steal Venezuelan resources. And for Western sheep-like humans, everything is alright and "Maduro is a dictator"! Come on!

Traitor Guaidó should be arrested in a democracy or dictatorship for calling to foreign military interventions and violent coups. He lives in a democracy where his party loses elections and then go to the streets using US money to call the death of democratically elected Maduro. Actually, Venezuelan democracy is too kind to him, letting him walk free while discrediting him. In the US he would be already arrested; probably being tortured. In many US-sponsored rogue states, he would be immediately tortured and executed. How mentally paralyzed are Western sheep-like humans to not come to this same conclusion: *Guaidó should be arrested but no, he keeps walking free[15], so there's no "oppressive dictatorship"?*

Origins and Connections

UCAB - Like most of the sector of Venezuelan society opposing the Bolivarian revolution (Catholic Church, Venezuelan private media, bankers, right-wing politicians, extremely wealthy families, right-wing racist intellectuals, etc.), Juan Guaidó studied at Andrés Bello Catholic University (UCAB), an infamous institution linked to Opus Dei and to all those who ruled Venezuela with strong deficits of democracy and who have been fighting during the last 20 years to have the Spanish-descent minority back to power and to regain the right to enslave the remaining majority as they used to do before Chávez.

George Washington University - Guaidó participated in two postgraduate programs in public administration at George Washington University, USA, where he learned neoliberal ideas from the Venezuelan economist Luis Enrique Berrizbeitia[16] who "previously held the position of Executive Director in the International Monetary Fund as representative of Spain, Mexico, Venezuela, and five Central American countries." No wonder one of the first things Guaidó promised after having declared himself President of Venezuela was to take out a loan with IMF. On January 25th, Reuters reported[17]:

> *"Venezuela opposition leader Juan Guaidó, who has proclaimed himself interim president with U.S. support, is considering a request for funds from international institutions including the IMF to finance his interim government, two sources said."*

CANVAS - In 2007, Guaidó and other students from private reactionary universities (the so-called "Generation 2007") started to get training from US-funded "regime change" organizations like CANVAS[18], with the financial support of oligarchs like Pedro Burelli. This organization is behind the training of thousands of people around the world to serve US illegal interferences in non-submissive nations. The people behind this seriously dangerous organization have mad ideas and have no qualms when it comes to present them, like 2010 Srdja Popovic's idea of sabotaging Venezuelan main damn[18], affecting 70% of the country's electricity grid, precisely what we witnessed a few weeks ago in Venezuela! No, there are no coincidences in the US's international acts of terror.

Yon Goicoechea - Another puppet from the "Generation 2007" and colleague of Juan Guaidó is Yon Goicoechea, who headed the campaign against the most democratic thing a citizen can participate: the 2007 constitutional revision. He became famous when the Venezuelan government declined to renew the license of RCTV, a television network deeply and directly involved[19] in the 2002 coup[20]. To compensate him for his attacks on fundamental rights of the Venezuelan people and crying out for a coup-plotter channel, Goicoechea was rewarded with Cato Institute's Milton Friedman Prize for Advancing Liberty, plus a $500,000 prize, enough money to buy plenty of C4 and machine guns for their murderous "democratic" uprisings.

As Dan Cohen and Max Blumenthal reminded us of[21]:

"Friedman, of course, was the godfather of the notorious neoliberal Chicago Boys who were imported into Chile by dictatorial junta leader Augusto Pinochet to implement policies of radical "shock doctrine"-style fiscal austerity. And the Cato Institute is the libertarian Washington DC-based think tank founded by the Koch Brothers, two top Republican Party donors who have become aggressive supporters of the right-wing across Latin America."

Yon Goicoechea was for a long period the most prominent figure of Generation 2007. Probably too prominent. Probably the reason why the US decided to illegally intervene in Venezuela using another puppet, Guaidó, as the chosen president. Eva Golinger, in one of her books, exposed many Goicoechea's links[22] to US "regime change" organizations and to the Venezuelan oligarchy. For instance:

"Goicochea traveled several times to Washington to meet with representatives of the National Endowment for Democracy (NED), the International Republican Institute (IRI), led by John McCain, and USAID, as well as the AEI [Albert Einstein Institution] and CANVAS. Goicochea traveled several times to Spain, Sponsored by the FAES[23] foundation of former Prime Minister José María Aznar, and to other countries, receiving funds from the United States as well as from neoliberal foundations such as Konrad Adenaeur.

Goicochea traveled to Bolivia during 2007 and 2008 to work and train the Cruceñista Youth Movement, the right-wing movement in the Santa Cruz area, Bolivia, known for its racist, violent and divisive attitude and actions. In May 2008, Goicochea was in Ecuador, training and encouraging the formation of a right-wing student movement in that country, Manos Blancas, to counter the socialist policy of Rafael Correa's government."

As you see, Yon Goicoechea gained experience in Bolivia, a country the US tried to balkanize in 2008-09, and in Ecuador, where the US made several attempts to remove Rafael Correa between 2008 and 2010. That's valuable know-out necessary to do more of the same in Venezuela.

Source 24 – Picture of Yon Goicoechea and Juan Guaidó together

Pedro Burelli - Guaidó is a violent protester backed by the Venezuelan oil oligarchy exiled in the US since Chávez rightfully nationalized Venezuelan oil. One of his sponsors is Pedro Burelli, a Venezuelan oligarch based in Washington, "who was once Head of Latin America to the J.P.Morgan Capital Corporation"[25], and was on the border of directors of PDVSA before Chávez nationalized it. Guaidó has daily phone calls with Burelli! Burelli has direct contact with the US administration, which he admitted in an interview podcasted by former CIA director Michael Morell. You can listen to the podcast here[26].

OTPOR! - OTPOR is a Serbian "regime change" organization backed by many US institutions like USAID, NED, NDI, IRI, IAE, Freedom House and others. Guaidó and his fellow coup-plotters are trained and guided by OTPOR personnel. OTPOR propaganda and actions successfully managed to get rid of Slobodan Milošević, as the US had ordered.

Their logo[27] in Serbia was a black hand with a white background (and also vice-versa). In Ukraine, the same logo but with an orange hand. In Georgia again the Serbian logo, but with the inscription in Georgian. In Kyrgyzstan the same, but with a rose hand. In Egypt, in Russia, in Iran, in Armenia, in Belarus and in so many other countries[28] where Gene Sharp-like *colored revolutions* and *springs* were attempted or even implemented, you can trace back OTPOR's links by checking the logos used by the movements injected from abroad. Right now[29], in 2019, the victim is Algeria with a red hand.

And yes, there's Mano Blancas (White Hands) in Venezuela, whose logo is an open white hand with black background (sometimes with the word "UCABistas", a reference to the religious right-wing university mentioned above, or "JAVU", a reference to a violent students' movement) or the same old Serbian logo but with the 3 colors of the Venezuelan flag.

In 2005, the American AEI brought 2 Serbians (Slobodan Dinovic and Ivan Marovic) to Venezuela to teach students how to weaken and disorganize power and how to build and handle a movement. In 2006, the students' movement trained by Gene Sharp, US Colonel Helvey and the OTPOR experts had its first organized action with the "Plan V", during the December presidential elections, but they weren't very successful.

"Plan V" was replaced by another action named "Movimiento Cambio" ("Change Movement" in English), also unsuccessful.

Success finally came in 2007, with the movement led by Yon Goicochea protesting against the government when this one declined to renew the license of RCTV. In October 2007, four Venezuelan students were sent to Belgrade to receive intensive training with OTPOR's experts: Ronel Gaglio, Geraldine Alvarez (UCAB), Rodrigo Diamanti (UCAB) and Eliza Totaro (UCAB). And so on. The connection between Venezuelan youth "opposition" and OTPOR, created by the US to dismantle and rape Serbia, is more than obvious.

Leopoldo López - Leopoldo López is one of the main mentors of Guaidó. On chapter 11, about the violent opposition, I already exposed the true criminal and terrorist nature of Leopoldo López. Like Leopoldo López, Juan Guaidó was directly involved in the 2014 "guarimbas" that resulted in great destruction of public property and in the death of many Venezuelans.

Yes, Guaidó was there with Leopoldo López when this criminal called for a violent uprising against the democratically elected Maduro.

Yes, Juan Guaidó actively participated in the 2014 violent uprising[33].

Guaidó's Agenda

Guaidó's agenda is a very simple one, and it is not his own. As previously said, he wants to bring IMF in, selling Venezuelan democracy to this organization known for its dirty tactics used to steal and enslave entire nations with austerity measures, privatization and shock therapies. On this subject of IMF's dirty actions, read *Enough Is Enough* [34], written by Davison L. Budhoo, a former IMF employee.

Guaidó officially informed the world that he plans to sell Venezuelan oil to foreign companies, namely US companies. Any doubt about it? No, he would not be president to serve the interests of Venezuelans. As he admitted, he would be president to serve foreign interests!

He admittedly despises socialism and affirms he is ready to do anything he can to get rid of socialism, even knowing the socialist PSUV party came to power thanks to a democratic process. He is not focused on the democratic process, he is focused on power as a mean to get more power (and money). His sick ambition and anti-socialism feelings are so great that he admitted he would be ready for Syrian-like bloodshed[35] as a mean to get rid of Maduro!

Like his mentors Leopoldo López and Henrique Capriles (who invaded Cuban Embassy during the 47 hours coup in 2002), Juan Guaidó manifests profound anti-Cuban feelings and ideas. Despite the fact both Venezuela and Cuba benefited immensely from their close relations and partnership, Guaidó declared that, as president, he would stop exporting oil to Cuba, joining the club of those who want to prove "Cuban communism doesn't work" by strangling it!

In one sentence, Guaidó's agenda is nothing but the US agenda of conquest, plunder, slavery, and destruction of the planet in the name of private "national interests".

Learn more

An easy and entertaining way to start digging out Guaidó's dark past and his undeniable links to the US criminal machine of illegal "regime changes" is to watch the interview of Lee Camp with Dan Cohen (Redacted Tonight VIP, episode 142[36]) as well as the episodes 230[37] and 231[38] of Redacted Tonight (also hosted by Lee Camp).

If you really want to learn in detail who Juan Guaidó really is, there's a superb article written on January 29th by Dan Cohen and Max Blumenthal. You can't afford to miss it: *The Making of Juan Guaidó: How the US Regime Change Laboratory Created Venezuela's Coup Leader* [39], [40].

Guaidó is nothing more than the 2019 version of Carmona[41], who in 2002 led Venezuela during the 47 hours of a US-sponsored and oligarchy-sponsored coup. The main difference between the two is that, so far, Guaidó ruled the country for *less* than zero seconds!

ANOTHER
FAILED COUP
21-27.06.2019

Sabotaged Electric Grid

On March 7th, 2019, an alleged cyberattack against Simon Bolivar Hydroelectric Plant (Guris Dam)[1] resulted in a general outage affecting more than 2/3 of Venezuela, mostly in the Western and Central provinces. Without a single piece of evidence, Western MSM immediately started accusing socialism in general, and Maduro's government in particular, of not "being able to manage a country". Strange, so well did the Bolivarian governments since 1999, even when it had to deal with US-sponsored oil lockouts and US-made electronic sabotage of their oil industry... And now, suddenly, we are invited to believe they are no longer able to manage the national power grid? Nonsense! Let's use our brainpower and try to figure out what really happened!

Source 2 - Satellite images of the Venezuelan territory before and after the electric outage

Yes, nonsense, otherwise, can someone in the Western MSM explain how did Venezuela recover so fast from the attacks against their electric grid? The grid was attacked on March 7th; on March 9th, power had been restored to most of the country, when a second outage occurred! Once again, Maduro's government complained about cyberattacks delivered from abroad. How can we blame his government for the outage? One week after the first attack, Venezuela had fully recovered from the electric outage. How can someone accuse Maduro's government of being unprofessional?

Furthermore, acts of sabotage are not new in Venezuela. Actually, they have been quite common in Latin American countries whose governments do not knee and do not obey US imperial orders. The US used criminal acts of sabotage on numerous occasions, trying to bend Cubans or successfully capturing Allende's Chile.

One year prior to this recent power outage, on February 15, 2018, an explosion at Santa Teresa 3 electricity plant[3] left most of Caracas without electricity. As always, MSM blamed Maduro's government. Maduro's government complained they were victims of sabotage coming from abroad.

In any case, one should not forget Venezuela has been suffering from a choking economic war, resulting in under-investment in strategic areas and a lack of funds to sustain proper maintenance and further investments. On top of it, the same US economic war on Venezuela creates fuel shortages that are also part of the problem. The New York Times explained[4] it very well, word by word:

"The sanctions have affected Venezuela's ability to import and produce the fuel required by the thermal power plants that could have backed up the Guri plant once it failed."

All this affected the Venezuelan people in different ways. People suffering in hospitals with no electricity, food losses, etc. To sabotage an electric plant serving 80% of the Venezuelan population could only result in disaster and human suffering. But, apparently, Guaidó, the Puppet, didn't seem to be very concerned with the resulting sufferance. On the contrary! He seemed to see it as one more useful weapon in the arsenal of planned "regime change" in Venezuela.

On the very same day (March 7th, Thursday) the electric outage took place, Juan Guaidó twitted[5, 6]:

"Venezuela knows the electricity will return once the usurpation ends. Let's move on. During our tour in the South, we sought support to address this crisis. We will overcome the blockade of progress with mobilization. See you on Saturday in the streets!"

Three days later, on a Sunday, he conveniently blamed Maduro's government for the power outage and for not being able to handle the crisis, recalling once again for the armed forces to act against the constitution and help him and his fellow coup-plotters removing Maduro, and announcing his intention to ask the National Assembly (controlled by the opposition) to declare a state of national alarm.

Happy or not for having Venezuelans dying in hospitals due to an electric outage, one thing we can be sure about is: he was not surprised. Why not? Because the "regime change" organizations behind Juan Guaidó and his fellow mercenaries had been talking for ages about electric outages in that very same Simon Bolivar Hydroelectric Plant.

As Max Blumenthal informed us on his article *US Regime Change Blueprint Proposed Venezuelan Electricity Blackouts as 'Watershed Event'*[7]:

"A September 2010 memo by a U.S.-funded soft power organization that helped train Venezuelan coup leader Juan Guaidó and his allies identifies the potential collapse of the country's electrical sector as 'a watershed event' that 'would likely have the impact of galvanizing public unrest in a way that no opposition group could ever hope to generate.' (...)

This group reportedly hosted Guaidó and the key leaders of his Popular Will party for a series of training sessions, fashioning them into a 'Generation 2007' determined to foment resistance to then-President Hugo Chávez and sabotage his plans to implement '21st century socialism' in Venezuela.

(...) Speculating on a 'grave possibility that some 70 percent of the country's electricity grid could go dark as soon as April 2010,' the CANVAS leader stated that 'an opposition group would be best served to take advantage of the situation and spin it against Chavez and towards their needs'."

The organization in question is called CANVAS, a US-funded group with experience on "regime changes". The memo was leaked by WikiLeaks and can be read here: *VZ elections*[8]. Unsurprisingly, in this memo, the names of Henrique Capriles, Leopoldo López and Yon Goicoechea are cited as "Key Players and Potential Allies". Once again, to see these persons as "political prisoners" is an example of Western irrational beliefs. An honest westerner seeking the truth, soon or later, realizes they are the very opposite!

Source 9 - Redacted Tonight - Episode 237

And a reasoning US citizens, soon or later, will realize Marco Rubio is a dangerous liar deeply involved with the people behind the blackout[10].

Rubio is a dangerous person and a liar, but he is not that clever, as he only waited 3 minutes before starting to tweet about the electric outage with details that no human being on Earth could be aware of, at that time, unless the power plant had been targeted by a planned act of sabotage and Rubio was well informed about it... in advance!

A few minutes after the blackout, when (supposedly) nobody knew absolutely nothing about the reasons for the lack of electricity, Marco Rubio was able to describe with astonishing precision what had just happened. As the Minister of Information Jorge Rodriguez noted[11]:

"Just a few minutes after the sabotage against our electrical system, he said: 'Reports of a complete power outage all across Venezuela at this moment. 18 of 23 states and the capital district are currently facing complete blackouts. Main airport without power and backup generators have failed.'

But look at one very important thing that this man mentioned and has to do with what we're going to explain immediately: 'backup generators have also failed.' How did he know specifically where the aggression was targeted? (...) How did he know that the backup generators, as he called them, couldn't work, if nobody knew about that just a few minutes after the criminal attack?"

Think about it!

Source 12 - Marco Rubio Knew Before About The Blackout- Jorge Rodriguez

*

It is obvious that those behind the sabotage had the intention to damage the image of Maduro's government. In the US, officials immediately accused Maduro and his colleagues of "incompetence" and "mismanagement". Nobody was interested in learning more about the power outage (probably because they already knew everything about it); they only wanted to attack and smear Maduro, as expected.

But Maduro reacted promptly, Venezuelan technician fixed the outage very rapidly, and two days later (March 9th), things were coming back to normal when a huge fire engulfed Sidor transforming substation[13] in the state of Bolivar. Apparently, something else had to be done to further damage Maduro's image and help Western prostituted journalists portraying him as a *dumb moron eating bananas*[14].

A few days later (March 14th), another substation was engulfed in fire in the state of Miranda[15]. As if, faced with the efficient reaction of the

Venezuelan authorities, the saboteurs had decided to continue with their acts of sabotage in order to prove their (wrong) point.

More than two weeks later, on March 25th, Venezuela suffered a second major electric outage, "with Venezuelan authorities denouncing a cyberattack similar to the one they claim caused a major blackout on March 7th, targeting the computerized system of the electric grid."[16]

Again, Venezuelan suffered a cyberattack.

Again, Simon Bolivar Hydroelectric Plant (Guris Dam) was targeted, with three transformers set on fire.

Again, more than 2/3 of Venezuela was left without electricity.

Again, the Venezuelan authorities and technicians were very efficient. As reported by Venezuelanalysis[16]:

"However, this time electricity was restored to Caracas within three hours and to the rest of the country after several additional hours when a second alleged attack took place at 9.50 pm. Reports emerged of a fire affecting three transformers in the Guri Dam switchyard, which then took out the San Geronimo high voltage transmission line."

Yes, you can conclude that it was more of the same. But do not forget Marco Rubio knew in advance what would happen with that "same" event.

One month after the second round of cyberattacks and acts of sabotage, the Venezuelan authorities arrested 5 suspects and informed 14 persons more are suspected of having participated in the attacks. One of those 14 persons is Jesus Landoni, ex-security chief of the Guri Complex who apparently left Venezuela and went to the US on April 8th, and who allegedly is now living "in a US Air Force official's house"[17].

By the time I was writing these words, most of what happened during the attacks had already been investigated, understood and explained in detail[18].

During his 75 minutes speech in Moscow on May 21st, Venezuela's Ambassador to Russia Carlos Rafael Faria Tortosa gave detailed information about the electric outages that occurred in March. For instance, he recalled the fact that never in the history of humankind, 20 generators malfunctioned simultaneously. It can happen to 1, although it is a very rare occurrence. Two generators malfunctioning simultaneously is incredibly odd. Statistically, it would be impossible to have 3 or 4 generators malfunctioning simultaneously. All the 20 generators malfunctioned simultaneously is, by itself, evidence of sabotage!

Watch the full speech[19] to learn more about the outages and other key issues like the many billions of euros *stolen* by European banks, preventing Venezuela from using its own money to buy medicines and medical equipment in the European market:

*

In a world where plenty of sheep-like humans in the US, Europe and elsewhere continue to believe in the fake story of "Russian interference in the 2016 US presidential election" after the Mueller Report[20] had already concluded it was fake... in a world where US media and US officials insistently accuse Russia of having "inserted malware that could sabotage American power plants, oil and gas pipelines, or water supplies"[21] without providing any single proof... somehow, we have The New York Times[21] and other media outlets calmly informing us, and therefore admitting, that the US does so in Russia:

"The United States is stepping up digital incursions into Russia's electric power grid in a warning to President Vladimir V. Putin and a demonstration of how the Trump administration is using new authorities to deploy cybertools more aggressively, current and former government officials said."

Amazing, no? Western sheep-like humans and all the other human beings alive are constantly invited to believe in unproven assertions about Russian interfering in the US undemocratic system or about Huawei spying god knows what! Western sheep-like humans, going against basic logic, swallow it. And then, when we have Americans proudly affirming they do interfere in Russia and they do deliver cyberattacks against Russia and they do commit acts of espionage in Russia... there's absolute tranquility about it among the usually paranoid westerners, as if they were living in a kind of dystopian blissfulness...

Every time something similar happens, I get more and more convinced that Westerners have definitely lost the ability to reason. And that's is the very reason why I decided to write this book.

But back to chapter 14, the subject is electric outages in Venezuela, possibly orchestrated by the US administration or by someone paid by the US administration to do so. I know, the skeptical reader is still waiting for hard pieces of evidence proving the US administration's fault. So do I.

But, in the meantime, let me remind you of two facts: first, the US administration was demonstrably involved in acts of sabotage and electronic warfare that occurred during the oil lockouts of 2002-03 in Venezuela; second, American officials and American media proudly admit the US commits cyberattacks against the Russian power grid[22]. Knowing so, how could someone be surprised with the US committing cyberattacks against the Venezuelan power grid?

Venezuelan Embassy Assaulted

After having recognized a guy (who was even not a candidate during the last election) as President of Venezuela, and while watching its dumb plans against Venezuela falling apart, one by one, the US administration decided to play a very dangerous card: to pressure Venezuelan diplomats to leave the Venezuelan Embassy in Washington and give room to "diplomats" representing the non-elected Venezuelan non-government kind of "ruled" by Juan Guaidó, a proven US puppet!

The Venezuelan personnel, following orders from the official government (of Nicolás Maduro), did leave the Embassy, not before inviting some of their North American friends to watch over the Embassy. These friends organized themselves as the Embassy Protection Collective[22] and remained inside the Embassy in full respect of the US law, the Venezuelan law and the International Law; if I am wrong please tell me why.

Not satisfied, the US administration continued to push, acting against International Law and US law, committing[23], ordering to commit and letting commit a series of crimes.

On May 8th, the same US that had attacked the Venezuelan electric grid decided to illegally cut off the electricity of the Venezuelan Embassy[24, 25], acting as a rogue state going mad.

Many Western Lying Media opted to downplay the serious incident, reason why they didn't bother to report the fact that the electric bill was paid[26] and that nobody had the right to cut off electricity.

The same happened with the water, illegally cut off[27], another act showing disrespect for the fundamental rights of the four US citizens still inside the Embassy.

The same happened with the access to food, another fundamental right of US citizens that was violated by the US authorities, who let anti-Venezuela thugs block those who repeatedly tried to deliver food to the persons staying inside the Embassy. Worse, in some cases, the very US authorities committed the crime of blocking that food while aggressing those trying to deliver it, proving once and for all that the US regime is not democratic. It is a fascist regime where authorities violate the law while preventing US citizens from acting in a lawful manner.

Unfortunately, Western sheep-like humans are indeed very sheep-like beings, to a point that nothing shocks them anymore if committed by Western rogue states.

If Russian or Chinese authorities would dare to commit such crimes, the very same oblivious Western sheep-like humans would lose their minds and would *immolate* themselves in frenetic acts of protest against the *devil regimes*... "Baa"!

Nowadays, in the US fascist regime, US citizens can be prevented from consuming food just because of some pro-Guaidó thugs physically blocking deliverers. Nowadays, in the US fascist regime, all this happens while the police forces actually help[28, 29] those pro-Guaidó thugs acting against US law on US soil!

Skeptical about these statements? Well, watch how pro-Guaidó thugs blocked food deliverers[30, 31] while the police forces were standing by. Watch how a deliverer is aggressed. Watch how the police forces protect the pro-Guaidó thugs committing felonies one after the other. Watch how the police forces decided to force the victim (the deliverer) to leave the area. All this can only happen in a failed state where the rule of law is no longer a reality.

No, seriously, in what kind of democracy the police would aggress and arrest a bleeding veteran of war[32] after his attempt to do something absolutely normal: to offer food to another fellow citizen? Are westerners in a collective coma or what? How can all these crimes and offenses occur with no signs of outrage on mainstream media nor on mainstream public opinion? Too many sheep-like humans around or what?

In what kind of democracy would the police arrest[33] one of its citizens for tossing a loaf of bread[34, 35] into an Embassy where starving activists wait for food and then charge her of "simple assault + throwing missile"?

Worse, independently of having committed or not the supposed felonies, in what kind of democracy would the police forces literally sabotage food delivering to four of its citizens? In a democracy, that's simply inconceivable! In the US, that's just normal. In the US, police forces destroy and take away baskets filled with food about to be delivered to activists inside the Embassy, proving the US is not a democratic nation.

Precisely because the US is not a democratic state, we had the opportunity to watch plenty of footage showing pro-Guaidó thugs and others attacking the Venezuelan Embassy, breaking windows and provoking other kinds of damages, with the US police forces passively watching their crimes. And we had the opportunity to watch pro-Venezuela activists being insulted, aggressed and even sexually assaulted, again with the US police forces passively watching. All this in the US failed state, not in democratic Venezuela.

Source 36 - Police are using some kind noise weapon to try to drive out the remaining folks in the embassy

*

All this is very symbolic. All this represent a small-scale version of what the US has been inflicting to Venezuela during the last several years: embargoes, sanctions, sieges, sabotages of the electric grid, starved people, Venezuela aggressed by US-paid mercenaries, attempted coups, etc.

But it doesn't end here. Of course not!

Unlike its Embassy in Washington, Venezuela didn't end up invaded by American military forces.

On May 14th, US police forces were about[37] to invade the Venezuelan Embassy, aware of the fact that to do so would be acting against International Law. Probably, this first attempt was just a futile attempt to scare the four brave activists and persuade them to leave the Embassy. Futile and pathetic. Inside and around the Venezuelan embassy, what was really happening was an ideological battle between American *idiocracy* and knowledgeable commitment standing for high and deep principles. The first ones, the creators and buyers of American *idiocracy* are now too far away from real reality. They can't even understand the very ideological and humanistic concepts in question, let alone analyze them, question them or accept them!

Two days later, on May 16th, US police forces finally did what they had been promising to do, illegally invading[38] the Venezuelan Embassy and arresting four US citizens[39] who committed no crime and who were Orwellianly accused of "illegal invasion of the Venezuelan Embassy" by US authorities actually doing so! Yes, absolutely Orwellian!

Now, these friends of Venezuela face charges for what they didn't do. They invaded nothing. They were invited by Venezuelan authorities to be there and lawfully remained there.

Their actual *crime* is to have dared to stand against the criminal behavior and the unlawful decisions taken by the administration of the rogue state they live in...

*

The moment the US administration gave orders to assault the Embassy of the sovereign state of Venezuela, they opened a Pandora Box full of dangerous surprises. The US administration set a precedent. Now, it has to pay for that and it will pay for that! Look at what just happened a few days after the American assault on the Venezuela Embassy: the US Embassy in Tegucigalpa (the capital city of Honduras) was set on fire[40, 41].

*

In order to fully understand what really happened during those days of criminal aggression against the US Embassy and against the members of Embassy Protection Collective[22], I highly advise you to watch 2 interviews Lee Camp made for his show Redacted Tonight VIP. In episode 154 he interviewed Ariel Gold from CODE PINK, a member of Embassy Protection Collective. In episode 156 he interviewed Margaret Flowers and Kevin Zeese, founders of Popular Resistance[42] and two of the members of Embassy Protection Collective that resisted until the very last day.

Source 43 - Redacted Tonight VIP – Episode 154 - Embassy Protector Arrested For Delivering Food
Source 44 - Redacted Tonight VIP – Episode 156 - Despite Arrest, Embassy Protectors Say They Aren't Backing Down

Another excellent resume of what happened is the article *US chose 'the violent and illegal path' against peace activists, Embassy protector tell the Canary*[45].

*

Finally, on May 24th, one week after the illegal invasion of the Venezuelan Embassy by the US authorities, pro-Guaidó supporters invaded and took control of it[46], an act that definitely officialized the United States of America as a rogue state! A rogue state so deranged and so lunatic that even dares to choose the personnel of foreign embassies!

General Figuera, Double Agent or Traitor?

Between April 30th and May 1st, Venezuela suffered a poorly attempted coup that could only fail miserably. Although counting only with a general and a bunch of low-ranked officials chaotically *organized,* for those watching Western Lying Media, the attempted coup had immense support from numerous high-ranked officials that were very well organized and were about to put a certain end to Maduro's "regime".

In postmodern journalism, "journalists" often report what they wish or believe, or what they are told to report, but not what is actually happening. When such levels of unprofessionalism are consistently maintained for long periods of time, shocking contradiction and blatant reconstruction of reality are unavoidable.

In the case of the failed coup in Venezuela, Western journalists went as far as starting to celebrate what was too far from happening, showing not only their profound lack of professionalism but also their total disconnection with reality.

*

As far as we know, General Manuel Ricardo Cristopher Figuera, director of Bolivarian Intelligence Service (SEBIN) plus some 50 officials attempted to trigger a military coup from La Carlota Airbase. At the same time, a few hundred of Guaidó's supporters rioted in the streets around the airbase. Nearby, in Caracas, some 3000 persons[47] joined a protest calling for a military coup. Juan Guaidó moved between the two coup stages, taking pictures and delivering delusional speeches[48], followed by a convicted criminal on the run named Leopoldo López.

Source 49 - Guaidó calls for a military uprising in Venezuela

According to Elliott Abrams[50] (a US diplomat appointed as Special Representative for Venezuela on January 25th, 2019), the US was counting on other 3 key Venezuelan figures to implement a US-sponsored "regime change". According to Elliott Abrams, on April 30th, when the coup attempt started, their "mobile phones were switched off" and he felt frustrated with the situation. Supposedly, one of the key figures was the Minister of Defense Vladimir Padrino López.

According to the US administration, the other 2 prominent figures from Maduro's "regime" were Maikel Moreno, the president of the Supreme Tribunal of Justice, and Iván Rafael Hernández Dala, Commander of the Presidential Guard and of the Directorate General of Military Counterintelligence (DGCIM).

Curious how the US administration has no qualms to admit its blatantly illegal interference in the internal affairs of a sovereign nation, no? The function of DGCIM is to prevent intelligence or espionage acts against Venezuela. The US administration had secret conversations with the head of DGCIM and, yet, there are still people on Earth breathing in and out and believing Maduro is the *bad guy* in this story!

The US administration admits having done so and the West is not shocked about it? Worse, some Western journalists even *whined, childishly,* upset with the outcome[51] of this US interference! Come on, seriously? Can't Western audiences and Western journalists realize how ridiculous and hypocritical is their position?

According to President Maduro and many others, including Western media and alternative media[52], General Figuera was a traitor who had been "recruited by CIA" and who, for one year[53], had been masterminding the failed coup.

Maduro affirmed that it was Padrino, Moreno, and Dala who informed him about Figuera's plan, one week before the coup. More, Maduro affirmed Figuera was fired and arrested on April 30th, reason why he would have aborted the planned coup. On the same day, he would have escaped and, apparently, nobody knows where he is now.

True or false this Maduro's version, the truth is the planned coup went on, but not as planned! Dozens of soldiers joined it, Leopoldo López showed up next to Guaidó and next to the coup-plotters who carried and fired machine guns against the police forces protecting the roads surrounding La Carlota Airbase. Were they simply misinformed or were they dumb pawns purposely drawn into the epicenter of a US-planned coup wisely counter-planned to fail? Both? Maybe.

Maduro made ironic remarks about General Figuera, noticing this general was not brave enough to join the riot at the airbase. A very good point!

But VoltaireNet sees it differently. In one of its reports[53], it is said that General Figuera gave false statements affirming there were several high-ranked officials ready to betray their government. In that case, General Figuera could have been absent not for lack of courage, but for being a double agent sabotaging the US-planned coup he was supposed to implement, right?

Source 54 – Picture of Nicolás Maduro and Vladimir Padrino

We don't know if he was a double agent pretending to be working on turning key figures of Maduro's administration against Maduro, but it would make all sense. It might be he was truly acting against Venezuela truly trying to turn key figures against Maduro. In both cases, overconfident US intelligentsia lost intelligence and can no longer organize coups as they used to do in the past. Venezuela and the free world are surely thankful for the rising *idiocracy* ruling the Empire!

General Figuera, as a traitor or as a double-agent, was supposed to convince Vladimir Padrino to sell his soul to the devil and side with the criminal aggressors in Washington. Extremely odd project this one of trying to have Maduro's right-hand man betraying the Bolivarian revolution, but why not.

With General Figuera betraying his motherland or, as a double agent, betraying the US plan to overthrow Maduro, and given all the facts we know about the attempted coup, the way the coup was attempted and its outcome lead us to conclude the US played the role of a laughable victim of a masterfully planned counter-espionage attack in which US coup-plotters were led to believe they had what they did not have: Venezuela key figures genuinely supporting a US-planned coup against Maduro. Consequently, misguided Americans decided to anticipate their whished coup, basing their actions on faked information and without real support to make it happen.

*

How could the US, with all the military technology and limitless budgets, possibly fall into such a trap? Good question.

If we analyze what Valentin Vasilescu[55] (a Romanian military expert) said[56], it might be easy to understand what probably happened and understand the reason why the Trump Administration was so overconfident and the Western MSM were so sure about a coup that was not happening at all.

Vasilescu affirmed the American would, in normal circumstances, use their surveillance program known as Echelon to collect and analyze Venezuelan Armed forces' communications in search of potential officials willing or ready to make part of a coup against the Venezuelan government. Somehow, several months ago, the Echelon surveillance program was blocked in Venezuela and it could no longer collect data potentially useful for the coup in the making.

Venezuela doesn't have the technological means to prevent Echelon from intercepting and collecting communications, but it happened. If so, somebody else did it. Vasilescu believes Russia or China were behind the electronic blockade, but he can't prove his assertion, and nobody will ever confirm it.

With no means to collect data for the preparation of its planned coup, the US administration had to go back to the old days and physically infiltrate CIA agents in the Venezuelan Armed Forces.

The Bolivarian Intelligence Service (SEBIN), aware of the US plans (How? Did General Figuera, head of SEBIN at that moment, inform the Venezuelan government as a double-agent would have done? Or was it the Russians or the Chinese who informed the Venezuelan government?), activated a counter-espionage plan, falsely presenting high-ranked officials as traitors ready to participate in the US-dreamed coup. These officials, with time, lead the US spies to believe that there were enough traitors to implement a coup. The Venezuelan counter-espionage tactics went as far as faking leaks from officials supposedly traitors, then offering the *leaks* to be published by local mainstream media (that are radically anti-Maduro).

The US fell into the trap and prematurely activated the plan to overthrow Maduro on April 30th. That was precisely what the Venezuelan government was praying for: an induced US-planned coup condemned to fail as a way to first, win time and be ready for a real one; second, discredit the local oligarchy and its puppets of "regime change"; third, humiliate the US in the international arena as a pathetic super-power unable to deliver a proper coup against a far weaker nation.

Unaware of the fact they had been led to act as the *jesters in a court*, US politicians, when faced with the *sad* reality, didn't know how to react or what to say. Lovely to watch the Empire appalled and speechless!

The Western Manipulative Media that had received orders to amplify and spread the extension and intensity of what was not happening, continue to act as if the coup was happening. So pathetic! Some of the less senile Western journalists were smart enough to mention "uncertainty" and "contradicting reports", but none of them working in major Western MSM were able to see the big picture and understand they were all trying to report, step by step, a coup that was not even happening. Lovely!

Guaidó, criminal on the run López and other puppets were also too far away from everything, completely oblivious, left with no clue about what was really going on. Look at their faces:

Source 57 – Picture of Juan Guaidó and Leopoldo López

*

During three consecutive days, I spent dozens of hours following live the coup that never was. I watched live broadcasts of several TV outlets from the Western World, from Venezuela (private and public) and from non-submissive countries like Russia. I focused my attention on Portuguese RTP, one of the major TV channels in my motherland and property of the Portuguese state. Portugal has a vast community of emigrants in Venezuela and, like Spain, is in the vanguard of Western propaganda against Venezuela. The bank that stole 1.5 billion dollars from the Venezuelan government (Novo Banco) is also Portuguese.

During two days, RTP journalists kept insisting the "revolution" (coup) was about to happen. Some of their journalists were there, in Caracas, a few minutes by car from the immense demonstrations organized by Maduro's supporters[58], but they didn't see it. Portuguese journalist Hélder Silva[59] was there, in Caracas, in the same square Guaidó made his empty promises to a few hundred of his followers. He reported live from Caracas, expressing his support to the illegal attempt to overthrow Maduro, clearly excited with the idea of watching Venezuelan being victim of an international crime. All this instead of reporting the truth backed by hard proofs.

RTP journalists in Lisbon kept talking about "huge crowds of Maduro supporters" and about a "majority of Venezuelans siding with Guaidó", but they were unable to provide footage to prove their odd *certainties*. Ironically, from what they broadcasted, everybody could see the streets around La Carlota Airbase practically empty[60]; the majority of the 32 million Venezuelans supposedly "siding with Guaidó" were absolutely invisible in their own footage.

The best RTP managed to do was to use a photo of a huge pro-Maduro demonstration as the cover of their website during the failed coup, next to sentences and articles transmitting the manipulated idea that the photo had been taken in one of those huge yet invisible pro-Guaidó demonstrations. The problem is the picture shows plenty of symbols that have nothing to do with Guaidó and his criminal opposition: portraits of Hugo Chávez, Nicolás Maduro and Simón Bolívar, and flags of Cuba and PSUV (Maduro's party)[61].

At the end of the second day, when it was already too damn obvious the US-planned coup had failed, RTP journalists were still talking about "uncertainty in Venezuela". As if they had decided to refuse reality. They were not the only ones. I witnessed the same in other Western MSM!

And even when the show had already ended, mainstream media's "experts" on International Politics or on Geopolitics could not figure out they had been fed by faked data provided by misguided US administration (their real boss). Blinded by their fundamentalism against alternative media and against Venezuela, they were, as always, preventing themselves from accessing information that could easily open their eyes and make them stop playing the foolish.

All these Western pseudo-journalists and pseudo-experts on international politics are so immersed in their little obscurantist world and so focused on their petty task of spreading Orwellian rhetoric against all those who do not submit to the Empire of Chaos and War, that they can't possibly realize how manipulated they are and how ridiculous they look in the eyes of awake human beings.

Neither the Western media nor the Venezuelan puppets, let alone the criminal US administration, understand why the Venezuelan people support the Bolivarian Revolution and why the US will never succeed in its attempts to overthrow Bolivarian governments in Venezuela.

The only way for the US to take full control over Venezuela and its resources is to carpet bomb this brave nation as they did to Laos in the 60s, and then invade it and finish the genocide recurring to US Army dead squads to slaughter the remaining Venezuelans. But such a crime can't be done in the 21st century (not that there is no desire on the part of Western supremacists) of worldwide real-time information, international institutions like the UN, anti-imperial forces growing stronger (Russia, China, Iran, etc.), Cuban wisdom, Bolivarianism, etc.

As it is not possible to commit sudden and massive genocides, the US is doomed to fail for the reasons Ángel Guerra Cabrera summed up[62]:

"The reason is that the revolution has deep roots in Venezuelan history and culture: Bolivarian, African, indigenous, peasant and worker struggles. It was cultivated with care by Hugo Chávez and his followers. The magisterium that the commander carried out from his weekly program Hello President, in his speeches and with the example of his life remained firmly rooted in the hearts and minds of Venezuelans. We cannot forget the practice of empowering the masses not only with the vote, but also with their influence in deciding the direction of the transformations. That is why Venezuela resists and why Trump and his puppets fail. Betrayals, like that of the head of Bolivarian intelligence, are not new in times of revolution nor do they change the destiny of any liberating enterprise.

I recommend you to watch this magnificent summary produced by redfish[63] about some of the reasons mentioned by Ángel Guerra Cabrera and about their obvious consequences[64].

*

Going back to Vasilescu analysis, this military expert argues that none of the nations bordering Venezuela (Guyana, Colombia, Brazil) have the necessary military means to invade it by land, and the geographical characteristics and lack of roads are not favorable in case of a ground invasion of the Bolivarian nation.

A traditional invasion with US marines landing in the shores of Venezuela would easily become a second Vietnam-like quagmire. Venezuelan troops are fully aware of this fact and sing it out loud[65].

To avoid such military quagmire, Vasilescu argues the only option left to the bellicose USA to military conquer Venezuela without killing its dozens of millions of inhabitants would be to organize a considerable coalition with its vassal states members of NATO.

The coalition would need to begin their intervention by delivering a systematic campaign of massive bombings against the infrastructure of the whole nation. Done so, they would have the required conditions to subdue the Venezuelan people and install a Pinochet-like draconian dictatorship, where all kinds of horrendous crimes would become a reality again; kidnappings, torture, the assassination of those resisting the US-imposed terror, etc.

But there's one *small* big problem: if the US destroys the entire Venezuelan infrastructure, neither the US nor the prostituted Western media will be able to claim humanitarian reasons as the reasons for Western *willingness* to intervene and "help the poor starving Venezuelans". The US would have material conditions to gain physical control of Venezuela, but the humanitarian farce and the media farce would fall apart.

As a result, the real reason for Western terrorism against Venezuela would be definitely exposed: to destroy a good and successful example of socialism. Yes, because what we have seen so far in our media is the exact opposite: they want to convince us that socialism does not work and that Venezuela suffers from hunger not because it has been the victim of years of Western sanctions and Western terrorism, but because supposedly socialism does not work.

So, like Cuba, Venezuela would only fall if the insane West would eliminate all Venezuelans.

Like with Cuba, the US needs to end with Venezuela, to get rid of a *bad* good example of socialism.

Like with Cuba, the US, because it cannot decimate the entire population of Venezuela, behaves like a vile *vulture ripping pieces of meat apart*, attacking Venezuela with sanctions, embargoes, sabotage of infrastructure, creation and sponsorship of terrorist groups, etc.

Like Cuba, Venezuela will continue to be the victim of the infinitely vile behavior of barbaric West.

Like Cuba has never fallen, Venezuela will never fall!

*

Well, without evidence confirming or disproving anything about General Figuera, let us follow the official version and accept that Figuera was indeed a traitor[66] and that the remaining three figures only pretended to support him in order to help sabotage the US plan and counterattack, leaving the Empire appalled and stunned.

After all, let's not forget the US administration, on May 8th (one week after the failed coup), lifted the sanctions[67] it had imposed on General Figuera when he has the head of SEBIN.

The Coup That Never Was

On April 30th, 2019, we were all invited to witness more of the same. Or so thought the US administration after having prepared the stage and the lights, and called the MSM to broadcast it.

The real US intentions in Venezuela are not a mystery and can be found in the 2002 coup against Hugo Chávez[68], when the US installed a dictator, suspended the Constitution and the Supreme Court and most of the Venezuelan administration.

As a result of past aggressions, good memory and excellent levels of education, Venezuelans as a whole cannot be fooled again[69] by the imperial US.

*

As Pepe Escobar affirmed in an interview to a Brazilian news outlet[70], Juan Guaidó was inside the Embassy of Colombia in Caracas when he called for a popular/military uprising against the legitimate government. Only then he went out and, in a small square nearby, faced his supporters. Apparently, Guaidó was not very confident or he is not brave enough to carry the responsibility of triggering such kind of crimes.

On the other hand, the Bolivarian government grew older, has experience as a victim of imperial aggression, and now knows how to face the aggressors. Venezuela no longer compromise. Venezuela no longer negotiates with governments behaving as organized mafias (USA) nor with their hitmen (Venezuela oligarchy, faked NGOs, etc.).

Moreover, the Venezuelan government followed and understood what happened in Libya and Syria: if you frame yourself with compromises to prove your good intentions, the aggressor will ignore your proofs of goods intention and will use your naive honesty to further frame you.

In Syria, 2011, al-Assad first reaction was not to send armed police forces against the Saudi-funded armed protesters coming from Jordan. As a result, Syrian police forces were slaughtered by terrorists. The West censored this fact. Only when al-Assad took the decision he had to take - to send armed forces -, the world was told al-Assad was slaughtering his people. Al-Assad got it, and so did Maduro.

Apparently, on April 30th, Maduro was being faced with a harsh *reality:* a military coup inside La Carlota Airbase, close to the capital city. Wisely, Maduro's government didn't fall into the perverted mediatic/humanitarian rhetoric of those who were precisely behind the potential bloodbath (the US and its vassal states) and acted firmly, promptly warning it would order the "use of weapons if needed as crowds of coup supporters flock to presidential palace"[71].

The Venezuelan Minister of Defense Vladimir Padrino Lopez immediately reacted to the threats of a military coup and, in a public statement, said:

"Anyone who comes to [the presidential palace of] Miraflores with violence will be defeated with violence. If we have to use weapons, we will use them."

Very well!

*

In the US, Marco Rubio (always him), ignoring the fact he is an American politician and Governor of Florida, started tweeting[72] his full support to a crime against sovereign Venezuela. Every single illegality is just normal nowadays in the US. Read what he had to say[73] at the beginning of the coup:

"This is the moment for those military officers in Venezuela to fulfill their constitutional oath & defend the legitimate interim President Guaidó in this effort to restore democracy. You can write history in the hours & days ahead."

*

In the Western world, MSM media were misinforming Western audiences about massive support to Guaidó's uprising that was not massive but tiny[74], and not an uprising but an illegal attack on a military base by a bunch of thugs armed with Molotov cocktails and guns.

Western Lying Media were transmitting pathetic fake news about "an airplane ready for Maduro to leave the country" and other nonsenses. I call it "fake news"[75] because unfounded reports of events that never took place, reported by pseudo-journalists who can't provide a single piece of evidence supporting their lies, are, literally, fake news.

This kind of psychological warfare is very well studied in Venezuela, a prime victim of US dirty tactics. Both the government and the Venezuelan people are well informed about it. In Venezuela, there are books like *Conjura mediática contra Venezuela*[76] (Media plot against Venezuela), *Psicoterrorismo Mediático - Una Amenaza a la Soberania Nacional*[77] (Mediatic Psycho-terrorism - A Threat to National sovereignty) and many others.

As expected, the Venezuelan people didn't swallow the Western tactics of psychological warfare and, to prove so, flooded the streets of the capital on April 30th[78] and May 1st[79] showing their massive support to the government they democratically voted for, although totally ignored by dishonest Western MSM.

Yes, plenty of people supporting Maduro on April 30th[80, 81]!

Yes, plenty of people supporting Maduro on May 1st[82, 83]!

And by the way, compare the peaceful pro-Maduro demonstrations with the violent behavior of the coup supports, events that were occurring simultaneously[84, 85, 86].

But the West is blind, the Western propaganda machine refuses to acknowledge that many human beings are awake and no longer swallow its vile lies.

Unsurprisingly, US Secretary of State Mike Pompeo doesn't get it either and, over excited, couldn't stop twitting and affirming shitty examples of psychological warfare[87]. And he was not alone. The US interference in Venezuela is not just criminal; it is also comic, laughable, pathetic, embarrassing, illogical; a grotesque mess orchestrated by many other idiotic terrorists like Pompeo[88].

The Venezuelan Minister of Foreign Affairs Jorge Arreaza gave him the right answer[89]:

"Making up fake news is a very sad way to accept that the coup you backed has failed... once again. Diplomacy has to be restored in the US Government.

Another silly lie of psychological warfare was Western MSM certainty of what was not happening: "Supporters of Guaidó guarantee that freedom has come to Venezuela", a title of a shameful report[90] by the Portuguese RTP in which, the only evidence shown was a guy saying so in front of Venezuelan police forces ignoring him!

This RTP's report is nothing more than manipulation serving the purposes of US psychological warfare, working to convince the Western population that "white is black", as a way to prepare them and buy their empathy for a potential criminal US aggression on Venezuela. We should have laws to lock these dangerous liars in high-security prisons!

RTP's journalists and other Western journalists can't even deny what I just accused them of, as they themselves publish absurdities proving they are aware of what they are supporting: criminal acts against a sovereign nation of a kind they would never accept to have in their own nations and would be the first to condemn such acts. I give you an excerpt of RTP's article as a perfect example:

"The objective of collecting funds would initially be to raise 40 million dollars, but in the next phase, the idea is to gain access to funds from the billions of dollars made selling Venezuelan oil, and from frozen accounts in several countries that have severed relations with Venezuela.

According to two sources cited by Reuters, Erik Prince, founder of Blackwater, is the main driving force behind the plan, who wants to organize 5000 mercenaries to fight for the self-proclaimed interim president of Venezuela, Juan Guaidó.

The mercenaries to be recruited should be Colombians, Peruvians, and Ecuadorians, all from Spanish speaking nations, because they are more politically acceptable than American mercenaries."

The title of this example of despicable Portuguese *journalism* [91] was: "Wanted mercenaries to fight for Guaidó". Do I have to explain what is wrong with this article and this title? I don't think so. Their own words made my point against them!

Similar news with the same shameful content can be easily found in English, proving that there's no plurality nor freedom of speech in Western Media. Western media simply copy-paste their bosses' scripts, while censoring or manipulating everything else.

- Blackwater founder's plan for mercenaries in Venezuela: Report (al-Jazeera)[92]
- Billionaire Blackwater founder wants his mercenaries in Venezuela to topple Maduro: report (Newsweek)[93]
- Exclusive - Blackwater founder's latest sales pitch: mercenaries for Venezuela (Reuters)[94]

Western MSM always have time to sell these kinds of Western projects of crimes against humanity, but they never find time to report the real crimes against humanity committed by the Venezuelan opposition on a daily bases. Fascist pro-coup Venezuelans beating up a supposed pro-government civilian while others call for his death, or the same fascists destroying communitarian centers, these are two examples of Venezuelan opposition crimes you will never learn about or watch on Western MSM:

Source 95 – Far-right opposition aggressing a man for supposedly being a Maduro's supporter
Source 96 – Social institution assaulted by far-right opposition, then set on fire

*

On the day of the planned coup, Juan Guaidó said plenty of nonsense[97]. Telesur highlighted[98] the most flagrant ones.

First, *Maduro doesn't control the Venezuelan armed forces.* Well, two months after the failed coup, the Venezuelan armed forces keep supporting the legitimate government, a fact, not an opinion. Maduro never lost control of anything, even during the failed coup.

Second, *the government has no support among the Venezuelan population.* That's a very well proven lie. Links proposed in this book offer plenty of footage showing huge crowds supporting the government they voted for, in contrast with the almost invisible supporters of Guaidó's criminal acts. Maduro got 2/3 of popular votes during the last presidential elections. Facts are facts.

Third, *the International Community supports Guaidó.* No, it doesn't. As already explained in chapter 12, precisely about the concept of "International Community", some 50 countries out of 193 inhabited by a tiny minority of the world's population does not qualify as "International Community". And anyway, even if so, even if the "International Community" was on his side, support for illegal and unconstitutional acts are worthless. A damn weak fallacy!

Fourth, *what was happening at that time could only be labeled as a coup if he, Guaidó, was the attacked one.* Nonsense. His postmodern speeches really go too far. He was not the president. He wanted to overtake power by overthrowing Maduro's government with the help of foreign forces. With fair or dumb reasons to attempt overthrowing Maduro's government, to do so would always make him a coup-plotter, never a victim of a coup.

Fifth, in Guaidó's opinion, *there can be no peaceful rebellion.* Nonsense. Peaceful rebellion happened in the past and some were successful. What one can't achieve is a peaceful rebellion without popular support. And that's precisely the problem he faced: lack of popular support. That's why he counted on foreign forces to help him triggering a violent "rebellion" against its own people. That's why he failed miserably.

In the very same day the failed coup started, Telesur published a list[99] of obvious facts disproving all the nonsenses Guaidó affirmed:

1. A small group of soldiers revolted themselves in collusion with the far-right.
2. La Carlota airbase and all military installations are in control of the national government.
3. Opponents blocked the Altamira Highway, a network of roads in the eastern part of the capital.
4. The Venezuelan government called on the people to gather in the Miraflores Palace (headquarters of the national government).
5. Different governments, parties, and movements around the world have rejected opposition violence in Venezuela, while far-right governments have encouraged it.

Two months later, when I write these words, and as always, nobody can deny the fact Telesur was right and Guaidó was wrong.

*

For those who followed the events with due attention, there was plenty of early evidence of a failed coup on the very first day it was attempted.

The coup-plotters shooting guns while affirming there were people shooting on both sides was an obvious example, very similar to what happened in 2002 in Llaguno Bridge[100]. Not able to take control of the airbase and trigger their wished coup, the coup-plotters recurred to the vile *Plan B* of playing the victims of their own criminal acts. There's no evidence at all of guns being fired from both sides. No, only from coup-plotters' side[101]. Facts are facts.

Thankfully, there's plenty of footage denying their assertions[102, 103].

Brave alternative journalist Dilyana Gaytandzhieva pointed out that, just like in Syria, "peaceful protests" showed up with guns and live ammunition[104], shooting at police forces with their American and

European guns. Meanwhile, Western MSM were accusing the very same police forces of oppressing those "peaceful protests".

American semi-automatic rifles AR-57[105] with silencers seen in the hands of heavily armed Guaidó's supporters in Venezuela, weapons supposedly inexistent in Venezuelan territory. Where did these weapons come from?

And what about the M4 Colt and the European FN MAG[106] also carried by coup-plotters?

Can someone explain how the coup-plotters from the far-right opposition got these guns, later left next to packs of bananas[107] on the highway surrounding La Carlota Airbase, in a clear and early sign of a failed coup?

To manipulate this early evidences of a failed coup, the criminal opposition counted, as always, with plenty of liars and dumbs American journalists. CNN broadcasted footage of coup-plotters firing live ammunition as supposed evidence of "regime" forces shooting on protesters. The problem is their own footage only shows "regime forces" carrying blue armbands[108] that only coup-plotters were using to identify themselves. Yes, CNN lied. No, CNN's footage doesn't show police forces under Maduro's control. CNN's footage shows coup-plotters and only coup-plotters firing guns! Facts are facts!

There was a very clear proof of what I just wrote, meanwhile censored[109] by the Western "free world"[110].

But let them erase their own lies, let CNN's Jake Tapper delete his own lies, as it helps to prove MSM media lie! Others, like RT, do not hide the truth they report and so RT's article exposing Jake Tapper's lies is still available[111].

Other early proofs of the failed coup were the speeches of the low-ranked officials who confessed[112, 113] having been brought into the coup thanks to false information and contradicting orders. They were told to show up for special ceremonies and only at the arrival they were informed of the plan to overthrow Maduro.

The behavior of condemned criminals like Leopoldo López also helped us to understand the coup had failed. Having disrespected the house arrest sentence to join the coup, Leopoldo López lied affirming he had been "liberated". Western MSM (Portuguese RTP included[114]) told us the very same lie, as if a condemned criminal on the run by his own conscious decision, could possibly qualify as an act of "liberation"! Dumb Orwellian Western media!

Hours later, we learned Leopoldo López was hiding in the Chilean Embassy, then in the Spanish Embassy, as Ricardo Vaz explained in his article *Venezuelan Military Putsch Defeated as Leopoldo Lopez Takes Refuge in Spanish Embassy*[115]. Yes, the coup had failed, although the next day Western MSM were still cheering for the coup to happen. Dumb Orwellian Western media!

*

Back to the subject of psychological warfare, during the 2 days of the failed coup, the US government and its obedient governments and media outlets in the US, Europe, and South American vassal states did all they could to damage Venezuelan image and misinform their citizens and audiences. I would like to highlight some examples of the mentioned psychological warfare:

1 - On April 30th, despite the fact that members of the US administration had clearly confirmed their involvement and support for the wished coup, and despite the fact the Venezuelan coup-plotters had clearly confirmed they were counting on illegal foreign intervention to help them, somehow, in a parallel reality of beings suffering of profound cognitive dissonance, Trump and other members of the US administration accused Cuba of being behind god knows what, somehow interfering on the US interference on the Venezuelan internal affairs! Even if it was true, an interference to undermine and interference would be far more acceptable than the first interference, no?

No, there's absolutely no case here against Cuba. Only imperial arrogance: the US administration, *pissed off* with their own incompetence when it comes to perpetrate crimes abroad, once again, turned its rage against the usual scapegoat and threatened Cuba with "full embargo and highest-level sanctions"[116].

2 - On the same day, Pompeo, Rubio and other US politicians accused Cuba of an invisible "intervention" of about 2000/3000 imaginary military forces! Even if true, would some 3000 imaginary Cubans be enough to stop the biggest military machine ever seen in human history? For instance, would some 3000 imaginary Cubans be enough to stop the 7 military bases the US has in Colombia or the almighty armada the US has in islands like Curaçao, neighboring Venezuela? Nonsense!

3 - On April 30th, in a pathetic example of Orwellian *newspeak*[117], US National Security Advisor John Bolton, commenting on the ongoing coup he worked for, affirmed that[118, 119] "this is clearly not a coup. We recognize Guaidó as the legitimate President of Venezuela". Do these people use a completely different *Newspeak*-English dictionary or what?

4 - Still on April 30th, fascist Brazil ruled by Jair Bolsonaro, joining forces with the American Axis of Evil (the real one), announced measures to destabilize its neighbor Venezuela[120], promising to hosts 70 Venezuelan deserters and offering R$ 224 million to provide emergency and humanitarian assistance for Venezuelans in Brazil. Bolsonaro's Brazil had no good intentions. Bolsonaro's Brazil was not trying to help to solve any problem, but rather fueling the US destabilization of Venezuela.

5 - On May 1st, in a traditional move to confuse Western audiences and make them believe stable Venezuela was about to collapse, the US administration barred "American pilots and low-flying planes from Venezuelan airspace"[121], citing "increasing political instability and tensions" as the reason for their Machiavellian decision. Bullshit!

6 - Also on May 1st, CNN misrepresented a guest's claim[122] and announced the most hilarious fake news of the coup: Russia had

nukes in Venezuela! Fake news after fake news and nothing of real news, that's what we have on "free" Western MSM!

*

Nothing about the real reality opposing their pre-made script, nothing about the massive[123, 124, 125, 126] support to Maduro's government. Has always, impossible to watch Maduro's supporters on Western MSM. Literally, millions supporting the government during the day of the failed coup and also on the next day, May 1st, the Workers Day, a very important celebration for true leftists.

The Western media were sure about "armed forces betraying Maduro", but no, it was not true. And there were plenty of proofs showing they were not. As always, Western MSM lied and hid the truth. It was impossible to have a military coup on April 30th, or on May 1st, or on the following days[127, 128, 129, 130, 131]. The Venezuelan government, alternative media[132] and alternative journalists broadcasted plenty of evidence showing the armed forces fully siding with the legitimate government of Venezuela.

The western populace didn't see any of this for many reasons: because Western media censored it; because Western populace was and is too lazy to search for it on alternative media; and also because the Western social media like Twitter were preventing alternative media and the Venezuelan authorities from using their accounts to inform us and expose the Western Media lies about the failed coup. For instance, during the failed coup, Vice President of Venezuela Delcy Rodríguez had her account temporarily restricted[133].

Venezuela is famous for fake news about "censored private media" that are not censored at all. On the other hand, Twitter and Facebook do censor Venezuelans, Syrians and Iranians all the time, but that is just fine for Western sheep-like humans behaving like sheep-like humans. No worries.

The Twitter that censored thousands of Syrian accounts, that censored thousands of Venezuelan accounts in the last 6 months of US interference in Venezuela, and that censored a few days ago 4700

Iranian accounts in synchrony with the latest round of US pressure on Iran, is the same Twitter that verified a new account for self-declared "interim president" Juan Guaidó[134]. How comes?

Do you want to talk about "interference" dear not dear zombie-like Yankees? So please talk about Yankee Twitter interfering in Venezuela affairs, not about "Russian interference" in US lame elections, an accusation already proven false.

*

At the end of the first day of the failed coup convened by Juan Guaidó, this petty US puppet was still dreaming about his "Operation Freedom", promising to continue the next day[135, 136]with his dumb and utterly failed plan against a Maduro who, according to the same Guaidó, had lost the support of the military forces (a big lie, as we witnessed on the following days[127, 128, 129, 130, 131]).

The "Evidence" of Repression

For many hours, I watched livestreams from Caracas, broadcasted by different kinds of media; Venezuelan private media, Western mainstream media, and alternative media. The raw footage shows the same real reality. The only difference is in the narratives of the journalists describing it accurately or not.

To those who haven't lost the ability to reason, the raw footage can help them to como to objective conclusions: the pro-coup "protests" were small in numbers; never the coup gain momentum; the coup failed from the very beginning; the pro-coup "protests" acted in an extremely violent manner, destroying and burning public and private property; only coup-plotters used guns to shoot real ammunition; the only "evidence" of police violence is an Orwellian manipulation of reality.

By only supposed evidence of police forces "oppressing protesters" I mean the incident of a police vehicle that hit a violent "peaceful" protester[137], an event the prostituted Western MSM broadcasted over and over! Nothing else to show, right?

I will debunk it but, but first, I recommend you to watch several livestreams[138, 139, 140, 141] recorded by media with completely different perspectives on the violent coup attempt. Dozens of hours of footage that, if watched, will easily convince a rational being that the incident was completely taken out of context for dirty propaganda purposes; for an anti-journalistic reason!

You can find many more[142] on YouTube.

On the other hand, because Western media totally ignored the huge crowds of pro-Maduro peaceful demonstrations, it is harder to find livestreams of those demonstrations. Thankfully, Ruptly (a Russian news agency) recorded part of it[143].

Now let's analyze the incident transformed by Western Lying Media in the single evidence of government "oppression" during the failed coup.

I watched the incident live. For hours I watched the police cars being attacked with fire, Molotov cocktails, and gunshots. Many hours of it, live on TV! For hours, tireless police forces never shot on the protesters nor attacked them. The far-right thugs didn't stop attacking the white police cars that were only driving in circles to prevent those thugs and criminals from approaching the airbase.

The only moment a policeman driving a vehicle lost control of it because of a bumper, suddenly, the West decided to see "evidence of oppression" where only happened an accident. Nobody died. Zero injured. The violent protester hit by the police car promptly stood up and ran away.

Nearby, there were plenty of criminal supporters of the coup shooting real ammunition against the passive police forces, a fact never mentioned by Western Lying Media. How can Western audiences not realize this narrative was completely flawed? For a tiny fraction of what Venezuelan criminal opposition did in the highway near the airbase, police forces in the US would have shot dead every single rioter! How can Western human beings not see the obvious truth?

A very easy way to prove Western MSM lie when mentioning "regime oppression" is to watch[144] footage showing absolutely passive policeman provoked by a protester calling for the invasion of the highway, near La Carlota Airbase, where protesters shot real ammunition against the police forces.

And now, to prove Western MSM are absolutely perverted and report manipulated facts to recreate their own fake narrative, please watch this video of Israeli forces hitting a Palestinian with their vehicle on purpose! Yes, on purpose, repeatedly, to then leave the vehicle and beat up the injured victim[145]!

And now I ask: where are the reports on the Israeli oppression of occupied Palestinian? Nothing? Western Vile Media didn't hear about this crime or decided not to report it, fearing their Zionist bosses would punish them?

Fearing bosses is not journalism. It is prostitution. And, by the way, double-standards are anti-journalistic!

One more example, from Colombia (aka Israel of Latin America)[146].

Again, unlike the accident in Caracas, the Colombian police forces hit several citizens on purpose, repeatedly, with their motorbikes! Not yet satisfied, vicious Colombian policemen tried to drive their motorbikes over their injured victims! Why wasn't this blatant example of Colombian police forces oppressing its people reported on Western media? Why?

Because Western Media's job is not to inform? Right!

Because Western Media duty is to lie, manipulate and deceive? Right!

So, what's wrong with westerners? Am I crazy or, definitely, I have the right to affirm Westerners have lost the ability to reason?

Apparently yes, Westerners have lost the ability to reason and became sheep-like humans!

Chronology of a Failed Coup Being Exposed

This long analysis of the US aggression on Venezuela is about to end. Not because the US administration changed its mind, but because, as expected, this latest *season* (January-May 2009) faded away after the humiliation the US suffered on April 30th. The only aspect left to analyze is, precisely, how it faded away, and how is Venezuela now, after half a year of aggression that faded away.

When listening to me firmly standing for Venezuela, many ask me the question: *How is Venezuela now, better or worse?*

My answer is always the same: *Venezuela is Venezuela, always the same, revolutionary, proud, firmly standing up. Venezuela will never fall! On the other hand, the vulture named USA, with infinitely more money and more firepower, and the will to damage Venezuela, will savagely continue to rip pieces of injured Venezuela apart, while it can!*

Venezuela didn't fall. Venezuela will not fall. But the savage US will not put an end to its criminal and evil behavior! Not now.

*

May 4 - Guaidó, The Puppet, informed the world he was considering the possibility of asking the US to intervene militarily in Venezuela[147]. Nonsense. First, that would be a crime. Second, he is not in a position to ask such a thing. Third, lucky him for living in an exceptionally open and kind democracy. In some Western democracies, we would be already arrested, at the least. In some real dictatorships, like Saudi Arabia, he would certainly be beheaded or crucified. Lucky him for being a citizen of one of the most democratic nations on Earth! *Too democratic* in this case!

May 5 - US Secretary of State Mike Pompeo announced the US was ready for a military attack against Venezuela and affirmed Trump has the authority to order such kind of attack without Congress approval[148]. Clearly, Pompeo despises US law as much as he despises International Law.

On the same day, CNN demonstrated the shitty Lying Media it is[149], reporting pathetic fake news: in CNN's parallel reality, elections were held in Venezuela in January 2019 and Juan Guaidó won it. In real reality, elections were held in Venezuela in May 2018 and Juan Guaidó was even not a candidate; Maduro won it with 67.8% of the popular vote[150].

May 7 - US Vice President Mike Pence announced new incentives to Venezuela's military to turn against President Nicolás Maduro[151]. Again, an example of US illegal interference in Venezuelan internal affairs. Definitely, the US is a shameless rogue state!

On the same day, brave yet peaceful Venezuelan journalists attacked Guaidó with words, accusing him of stealing the nation and trying a coup against its legitimate government[152]. Why can't we watch on Western MSM these stubborn Venezuelan journalists doing real journalism? Simple, because in Western MSM there's no room for true journalism! And, by the way, showing the head of a failed coup walking free while being interviewed by Venezuelan journalists attacking him, well, it would surely damage the fake narrative Western MSM have on Venezuela!

Also on the same day, Vice President of the National Assembly Edgar Zambrano was targeted[153] by those same stubborn Venezuelan journalists who asked him if, in the next coup attempt, he would use ripe bananas or unripe bananas, an allusion to the famous photo showing abandoned guns and bananas after the failed coup[107]. The word "ripe" in Spanish is also the surname of the Venezuelan President: Maduro.

May 8 - Venezuelan Embassy in the United Kingdom denounced the suspension of its Twitter account[154]. No, there's no "freedom of expression" in the West.

May 9 - Vice President of the National Assembly Edgar Zambrano was finally arrested, after having participated in a coup attempt. He did it openly; it was recorded by many media. Yet, Western Media, like Portuguese RTP[155], were outraged with this latest victim of "Venezuelan oppression". As if the Portuguese authorities would have waited eight days to arrest a Portuguese citizen caught trying to overthrow the Portuguese government! Come on!

According to Western Media[155], the US, the Lima Group and the so-called "International Community" repudiated the decision. Sure, why not. By definition, Western Media repudiate legality in Venezuela, while supporting criminal acts against its people and its government.

But do you remember the 2016 Turkish coup d'état attempted against Erdogan? Were the coup-plotter arrested? Sure they were, all the coup-plotters plus thousands of innocents! During the coup, hundreds of people were killed and thousands injured[156]. According to Wikipedia[157]:

"Mass arrests followed, with at least 40,000 detained, including at least 10,000 soldiers and, for reasons that remain unclear, 2,745 judges. 15,000 education staff were also suspended and the licenses of 21,000 teachers working at private institutions were revoked as well after the government alleged they were loyal to Gülen. More than 77,000 people have been arrested and over 160,000 fired from their jobs, on accusations of connections to Gülen.

Back then, Western Media pretended to be appalled by such unprecedented and shocking levels of repression but were shy to report details. Eventually, Western Media *forgot* this issue for good. So now, please, don't tell us lies about "political prisoners" being "repressed by the Venezuelan regime". Give us a break!

Venezuelan authorities issued arrest warrants for eight people, but did it quite late, giving them time to seek political asylum in several embassies. In Turkey, 77,000 persons were arrested with no direct link to the coup. Give us a break!

On the same day, reacting to the detention of Edgar Zambrano, Juan Guaidó asked[158] the "International Community" for help. Sure, why not.

May 10 - Nicolás Maduro criticized[159] the Portuguese bank Novo Banco, affirming: "They stole us in Portugal"[160], while asking the Portuguese government to help returning the stolen money[161]. The

Portuguese government, *kissing the ass* of its Yankee boss, ignored Maduro's request.

On the same day, Juan Guaidó declared he could "accept" a US intervention in Venezuela[162], as if he was in a position to accept such a thing!

May 11 - Venezuelan Navy expelled the US navy ship USCGC James from its territorial waters[163, 164]. Another example of illegal intervention proving the US is indeed a rogue state.

Also on May 11, Juan Guaidó officially requested US military support[165, 166]. Can Western MSM acknowledge the fact the US systematically intervenes in Venezuela? Can Western MSM acknowledge the fact Juan Guaidó begs to be arrested? No, they can't!

Guaidó even affirmed that a US intervention in Venezuela was about to happen[167], only for Western Media to continue to see him as a victim of "persecution".

Also on May 11, 170 Venezuelans returned from Ecuador[168] thanks to Plan Vuelta a la Patria, a project to bring emigrants back to Venezuela. When Venezuelans move in (and not out), Western Media stay silent, in a clear demonstration of anti-journalistic double-standards.

May 12 - Corina Machado, a Venezuelan politician involved in many illegal actions against the Venezuelan government (read chapter 11), decided to speak out and admit[169] that the Bolivarian government she fought against for so long "is not a dictatorship"[170, 171] and it is a "huge error" to claim otherwise. According to Corina Machado, "in Venezuela, there's an unconventional war". Exactly! She took a lot of time to realize it, but better late than never!

May 15 - "Guaidó's 'envoy' set to meet Pentagon officials to plan ways of bringing 'democracy' to Venezuela"[172], as previously requested.

May 16 - The US, acting against International Law, decided to invade[173] the Venezuela Embassy in Washington, assaulting it with 100 armed forces to arrest the remaining four US activists legally[174] staying there.

For the US rogue state, the *Vienna Convention on Diplomatic Relations*[175] is some kind of toilet paper:

"Vienna Convention on Diplomatic Relations
Article 31
INVIOLABILITY OF THE CONSULAR PREMISES
1. Consular premises shall be inviolable to the extent provided in this Article.
2. The authorities of the receiving State shall not enter that part of the consular premises which is used exclusively for the purpose of the work of the consular post except with the consent of the head of the consular post or of his designee or of the head of the diplomatic mission of the sending State. The consent of the head of the consular post may, however, be assumed in case of fire or other disaster requiring prompt protective action."

On the same day, the US administration ordered the "suspension of flights between the US and Venezuela"[176], another chapter added to the psychological warfare. Ingenious Venezuelans immediately found and spread solutions to bypass the measure recurring to stopover flights.

Also on May 16, the first round[177] of negotiations between the Venezuelan government and the opposition took place in Oslo. According to Venezuela's Ambassador to Russia Carlos Rafael Faria, the opposition abandoned the meeting without establishing any kind of negotiation.

Also on May 16, Guaidó claimed to be in control of CITGO, a Venezuela's US-based PDVSA subsidiary[178].

May 17 - Venezuela and Russia started negotiations to drop the US dollar in bilateral trade[179] and replace it with the Russian ruble.

Also on May 17, a US judge ordered the release of the four activists arrested[180] at the Embassy of Venezuela in Washington.

May 18 - An iconic example of inexistent support for the many Guaidó attempts to reenact his pathetic failed-coup[181] took place in Venezuela.

The "majority of the population supporting Guaidó", as RTP journalists and many others constantly report, is clearly a lie!

Also on May 18, Portuguese RTP reported[182] the EU came out with a dumb (and old) solution for the Venezuelan crisis: new presidential elections! EU, a dictatorship were leaders are nominated instead of being elected, proposes presidential election in a country where presidential elections were held 1 year ago. What a dumb proposal!

May 20 - US National Security Advisor John Bolton[183] came out with one of the best examples of Orwellian *newspeak* ever pronounced. By "democratically elected" Bolton means "chosen by the US administration" or what? Guaidó was even not a candidate during May 2018 presidential elections! Given the fact Maduro was elected, his government can't possibly be a "dictatorship". Dumb Bolton!

Also on May 20, Maduro *fired* a brilliant diplomatic *counterstrike,* proposing early elections for the opposition-held National Assembly[184]. If the opposition, supported by the US and the EU, really want to have elections, and given the fact presidential elections can't be held now, why not accept Maduro's invitation and risk their majority at the National Assembly? Ah, brilliant. With this move, Maduro proved the Venezuelan government doesn't fear democratic elections, while forcing the opposition to admit they do fear elections. Brilliant!

May 21 – Venezuela's Ambassador to Russia gave a long press conference that everyone interested in the subject of this book should watch[185].

May 23 - We learned that from May 10 to 17, and for the first time in weeks, the US imported 49,000 barrels of crude[186] from Venezuela.

May 24 – Lee Camp, in episode 245[187] of his TV show *Redacted Tonight*, explained who anti-Maduro protesters outside the Venezuelan Embassy in Washington are artificially created.

May 27 - Guaidó took control over the Venezuelan petrochemical company Monómeros Colombo Venezolano[188], based in Colombia.

May 30 – We learned the second round of diplomatic talks in Oslo[189], once again, ended without a deal.

June 7 - In a leaked audio conversation[190], Mike Pompeo commented on the hardship of dealing with the Venezuelan "opposition" in the process of selecting a new leader[191] to be imposed as President of Venezuela. What a perfect example of illegal US intervention on Venezuelan affairs[192]!

*

With all this information widely available, I am asking one last time: why can't westerners acknowledge factual reality as it is?

Not enough facts? No, there are already too many facts to prove Venezuela is a victim of multi-dimensional aggression coming from a rogue state named USA.

Not enough historical examples of the very same kind of aggression? No, again, there are already too many in almost all Latin America nations and in many other nations like Iran 1953[193] or Indonesia 1965[194].

Westerners do not know what is going on in Venezuela because westerners simply refuse to know what is going on in Venezuela and prefer to believe in a parallel reality.

Yes, believe, that's the word, "to believe", as the opposite of "to know".

Westerners do not want to know!

So, again, what's wrong with westerners? Am I crazy or, definitely, do I have the right to affirm westerners have lost the ability to reason?

Yes, westerners have lost the ability to reason!

ABOUT THE AUTHOR

Luis Garcia is a Portuguese citizen, born in a small conservative village in the Portuguese seaside, where he lived until the age of 18. He never let himself be persuaded by *clichés* or definitive *truths,* cultivating since his early years of life the passion of reading and a rebellious willingness of self-education in search of the most inconvenient truths that are never pronounced.

Luis Garcia traveled in 56 countries, lived in 10 of them (including countries such as China, Lebanon or Lithuania), and is currently based in Thailand. The purpose of his travels is and has always been to merge himself with local realities in order to perceive the real problems that afflict the peoples of this world.

Because Western terrorism of plunder and genocide is an obvious reality in almost every country he visited and lived in, it would be impossible for him not to notice the terrible, suicidal and dystopian path towards which we are all blindly marching. This is the reason why the author moved from the perception of the surrounding reality to the constant exposure of this dystopian reality. That is why he writes political analysis essays (especially on Syria and Venezuela, and on the systematic production of lies by the Portuguese disinformative media).

That is why he reads and translates essays from brilliant and brave individuals such as Eva Bartlett, Vanessa Beeley, Tim Anderson, Sarah Abed, and others. These rebellious writers, researchers, and independent journalists, like few, manage to accurately and objectively define and report the reality the overwhelming majority of Westerners, for absolutely selfish reasons, choose not to know about. Luís Garcia translates their work into Portuguese as an extension of his own researching work.

His essays can be read on the website **Pensamentos Nómadas** (in Portuguese), on the website **Nomadic Thoughts** (in English) and on the website **Pensées Nomades** (in French), all of them created and managed by the author of this book. On the website **Pensamentos Nómadas**, you can also find his translations of articles and essays written by the authors mentioned above.

Website: https://nomadicthoughts.blogs.sapo.pt/
Twitter: @lgnomada

www.ingramcontent.com/pod-product-compliance
Lightning Source LLC
Chambersburg PA
CBHW072039280526
45788CB00006B/2115